DIS

Kodak Guide to

Shooting Great

Travel Pictures

Kodak Guide to Shooting Great Travel Pictures

HOW TO TAKE TRAVEL

PICTURES LIKE A PRO

by Jeff Wignall

Fodor's Travel Publications, Inc.

New York • Toronto • London • Sydney • Auckland

Grateful acknowledgment is made to Eastman Kodak Co. for permission to use its photographs reproduced herein, as well as to Alida Beck, Peter Guttman, Catherine Karnow, Boyd Norton, Ray Sarapillo, and Jeff Wignall for their photographs. A list of photo contributors appears on page 213.

Kodak Guide to Shooting Great Travel Pictures

Creative Director: Fabrizio La Rocca
Design: Alida Beck
Cover Design: Alida Beck
Cover Photos: Peter Guttman, Boyd Norton, and Ray Sarapillo, and courtesy of Eastman Kodak Company.
Color Production: Tigist Getachew, Carol Nelson
Film Generation: North Market Street Graphics, Lancaster, PA.
Production Coordination and Purchasing: C.R. Bloodgood, R. Shields
Photo CD processing: AppliedGraphics Technologies, NY, NY.,

Special Sale

PRINTED IN CHINA BY TWIN AGE LTD.
10 9 8 7 6 5 4 3 2 1

˙˙˙˙ Contents

Introduction *viii*

Human Places, Human Faces *1*

Natural Places, Wild Faces *41*

Light, Weather, and Natural Phenomena *85*

Introduction

This is a book for people who like to travel and who like to take pictures of the places they visit—a group of which I am happy to be a member. Whether you travel to rationalize shooting lots of film or your photography habit drives you to find new places to shoot, and whether you're an experienced SLR photographer or a casual point-and-shooter, this book is meant for you.

It is a book as much about how to find and approach different subjects as about camera settings. Many of the concepts discussed can be realized with the simplest point-and-shoot cameras, but where the SLR shooter would benefit from specific information about apertures and shutter speeds, I have included them.

Because travel itself is such a broad subject, covering everything from a Saturday drive to a round-the-world cruise, I have approached travel photography through both broad themes and specific topics: by types of subjects (landscapes, architecture, portraits, animals), by shooting conditions (humidity, rain, dramatic lighting), by compositional devices (horizon placement, frames-within-

frames), and by camera technique (exposure, depth of field, filters, camera choice). Being aware of and making the connections between these four image building-blocks— and applying them to your own situations—should enable you to see consistent (and relatively rapid) improvement in your travel pictures. Knowing, for instance, that you can use a long shutter speed to blur the rushing waters of a waterfall and a wide-angle lens and low shooting angle to accentuate its height can mean the difference between a casual snapshot and a remarkable picture.

The photographs are from several sources, including my own files, as well as the extensive picture collection of Eastman Kodak—a great number of which were shot by amateur picture-takers.

In addition, I am very pleased that we are able to present special portfolios by three of the world's premiere travel photographers: Peter Guttman, Catherine Karnow, and Boyd Norton. These portfolios are intended to give you an idea of what a talented person with practice and persistence can accomplish. Nothing they do is beyond what you can aspire to.

In one important way, producing this book has been an experiment: it is one of the first (if not the first) heavily illustrated books to be published using Kodak's new Photo CD technology. Each photograph in the book, whether it originated as a color (or black-and-white) negative or color slide, was transferred digitally to an optical Photo CD (CD Rom) disk. All of the color correcting, sizing, and sharpening of the images on these pages was done on a desktop computer under the direction of Fodor's creative director, Fabrizio La Rocca. It was a pioneering leap in book publishing in the digital age and it is in no small part Fabrizio's dedication that made this project a reality.

Thanks also to Nancy van Itallie, my editor, for her tireless efforts on behalf of the book. Thanks as well to photographers Peter Guttman, Catherine Karnow, and Boyd Norton for contributing their time and photography; to Jeff Pollock, president of Silver Pixel Press; and to Derek Doeffinger at Kodak for his help in conceiving the book.

Listed in Further Reading (page 212) are some of the books that have helped me in learning about photography. You'll probably find them at your local public library, which is, coincidentally, a great place to begin researching your next trip.

Human Faces, Human Places

1

City Streets

Although I always seem to daydream about restful rural places when I'm planning a trip, the place I like to photograph most is the city—any city. For sheer variety of subjects—architecture, interesting faces, open-air markets, historic landmarks,

parks—nothing competes with the urban whirl. Best of all, you can change subjects as your mood or your ideas evolve and usually just by turning another corner. In Manhattan, for instance, the glamour of the United Nations, the glitz (and grunge) of Times Square, and the cool shade of Central Park are mere blocks apart.

Unlike zooming through the countryside in a car at warp speed, hoping that a wonderful vista will pop up beside you, trekking a city's streets immerses you in its most intimate details. The kind of photographs you're likely to find will depend a lot on the personality of the city. If your stay is brief, take a short bus tour to find out exactly where you are and hatch some good picture ideas.

In cities where old and new live shoulder to shoulder, look for scenes that reveal that contrast: In the photo at right, I used a 28 mm wide-angle lens to contrast the gothic architecture of St. Patrick's Cathedral with a modern steel and glass Manhattan skyscraper. In frenetic hubs like Tokyo or London, you can catch the energy by using a very long telephoto lens (see page 172) to compress crowds or a long exposure (see page 162) to intentionally blur the bustle.

Whatever the locale, an advantage of city photography is that you can—and should—travel light with respect to equipment. A point-and-shoot or SLR that provides autoexposure and autofocus will free you to concentrate on your compositions and enable you to respond quickly to picture opportunities. A zoom lens in the 28 mm to 85 mm range will embrace wide views and still let you close in on interesting faces or architectural details.

Focal Points

- **Take a bus or walking tour to get acclimated**
- **Explore markets, streets, and parks**
- **Travel light so you can shoot quickly**

2

City Vistas

Cities that seem chaotic and intense up close often appear surprisingly elegant and orderly from high above or viewed from a distance. From on high, patterns emerge in the grids of streets and rows of buildings that are all but invisible at street level; distant shots often reveal a graceful skyline.

The most difficult part of photographing cityscapes is finding vantage points. Most major cities have observation decks that offer good overviews. Or, if you're lucky enough to get a hotel room on an upper floor (I always make it a point to ask for one), you can shoot from your own or a hall window (turn off the room lights to keep reflections down if you have to shoot through the glass). Surrounding hills and bridges provide good vantage points for more expansive views, such as the classic views of San Francisco shot from across the bay.

Midday pictures are usually pretty dull, but twilight shots (within 10 to 20 minutes after sunset) are especially glamorous because there is plenty of blue light left in the sky and the buildings and streetlights have begun to glimmer. A few moments before sunset, try to shoot *from* the west to catch the last rays of the setting sun igniting the skyline. Use a fast film (ISO 400 or 1000) to provide a shutter speed that's safe for handholding (1/60 second or faster; see page 188).

At dusk or dawn, the contrast of the bright sky and dimmer buildings can make it difficult for your camera to judge the correct exposure; but color print film usually has enough latitude to provide acceptable results over a range of exposures. For insurance, particularly when you're using slide film, which is less forgiving for wrong exposures, use your exposure-bracketing feature to make exposures at one and two stops over and under the recommended setting and take notes for future reference.

Focal Points

- **Find high vantage points to reveal city views**
- **Shoot early or late in the day**
- **At twilight, use fast films and bracket exposures**

Royal Dwellings

Like settings from a fairy tale, castles, palaces, and other royal abodes stir the imagination with their grand and often fanciful architecture. Though the Gothic stone castles of Europe differ wildly from the ornate palaces of Asia, the challenge of photographing both is to capture their spirit of fantasy and history.

Many royal buildings—the castles along the Rhine in Germany, for example—were designed by their architects to appear imposing from great distances. One way to photograph them is as you first see them: rising through the mist like apparitions. Medieval castles were also designed to be as inaccessible as possible, so look for angles that reveal the inhospitable surroundings and the drama of their location. A medium telephoto lens (85 mm to 135 mm) will enable you to capture both structure and surroundings from a distance. From nearby, use a wide-angle lens to exaggerate the height of sheer rock walls or steep cliffs.

The other alternative, of course, is to tour the building and photograph it in all its royal detail. Close-up views of turrets or, in the case of an ornate palace, colorful carvings or mosaics make interesting subjects. If the building is open to the public, a tour may give you some strong visual opportunities looking from the inside out. Use a very wide angle lens (28 mm), and try framing other parts of the building through windows or doorways, as in the shot at far right, or show distant views as they're seen from within.

The main problem you encounter photographing from nearby is keeping signs of the 20th century out of your pictures. A parking lot full of tour buses doesn't do much to enhance the romance of a medieval castle. Of course, you could include such modern juxtapositions to make a less idealistic statement. Don't be discouraged either if the weather turns sour. Storm clouds, rain, fog, mist, and snow often dramatize the settings and heighten the fantasy of such regal scenes. If the buildings are artistically lit, night shots can produce dramatic results, but bring a tripod to keep the camera steady during long exposures.

Focal Points

- **Work from a distance to reveal setting**
- **Move close to capture telling details**
- **Use weather and lighting to establish mood**

Formal Gardens

Formal gardens provide a great opportunity to create some stunning landscape photographs. Beautiful public gardens exist in virtually every part of the world and are usually a microcosm of the geographic location itself. The meditation gardens of

Japan or the plantation gardens of the American South provide evocative reflections of their locale. Equipment isn't much of a factor; a point-and-shoot will provide fine results. Because much of the design work has been done for you and the area involved is relatively small, you can often capture many different views in just a short visit. If the garden has very formalized rows of flower beds, a high angle (from a porch or hillside) will reveal their patterns. At ground level a wide-angle lens will help exaggerate the perspective of long flower rows. In more free-form settings, try to build

your compositions around a single feature: a particularly interesting piece of topiary or a river of stone winding through a meditation garden.

Gardens at peak season will, of course, provide the most colorful and extravagant pictures, but go early in the day to avoid crowds and trampled footpaths. If your travels take you to a garden that is prior to or past its peak, concentrate on wider views that rely less on individual flowers or plants and more on the landscaping itself. The one day I had to visit the Magnolia Plantation and Gardens outside Charleston, South Carolina, the peak had already passed and it was pouring rain. Putting (most of) my disappointment aside, I concentrated on compositions that revealed other aspects of the garden: footbridges reflected in misty pools, individual buds dripping with rain. A bonus was that my companion and I were the only visitors in the garden.

Focal Points

- **Exploit high angles to show garden design**
- **Use wide-angle lenses to exaggerate depth and distance**
- **Arrive early to beat crowds**

Landmarks and Monuments

The problem in photographing most famous landmarks is that, well, they're famous. So famous, in fact, that almost any photo of them—even a particularly clever one—is in danger of being viewed as a visual cliché. The challenge, then, is to bring home a souvenir picture that's both identifiable (you want people to know where you were) and also a creative notch above the postcard view.

Don't, however, discount the postcard view too quickly. Whenever I arrive in a new city or country, the first thing I do is raid the postcard racks to see how other photographers have interpreted local landmarks. Then, before I begin the search for more personal or creative interpretations, I steam through a few rolls rephotographing those views. This way, even if I never find *the* creative image, I've still got something to show for my efforts.

You can find alternatives to ordinary views by scouting around for unconventional vantage points. We all know what the Golden Gate Bridge looks like from the famous hillside overlook, but how about walking down by the bay and shooting up from underneath? Or framing it through the rear window of a cab in rush hour traffic? Odd juxtapositions have potential, too—the more unexpected the better. Everyone is familiar with the pristine views of the Statue of Liberty, but how many photographers explore it from the New Jersey shore of the Hudson and include tugboats or decaying barges in the foreground?

There are no rules either that say your pictures have to show all of a landmark or provide an entirely literal interpretation. Sometimes isolated pieces of a subject are more visually arresting than the whole and just as identifiable. Try using a long lens (200 mm) or zoom to close in on Lincoln's face at his Washington, D.C., monument, for instance. Lastly, don't overlook abstraction, as in the reflection of the Washington Monument in the glossy face of the Vietnam Memorial in the photo at right.

Focal Points

- **Review postcard racks for traditional views**
- **Seek out distant or unusual views**
- **Look for interesting vignettes or details**

Houses of Worship

In addition to reflecting their deepest spiritual beliefs, the places where people worship are often signposts of architectural and social progress. Pictures of them, both inside and out, can make an excellent running theme in your travel album.

One common frustration travelers encounter in photographing such buildings is getting a clear shot at them. Often nearby vantage points are obscured by other buildings or the clutter of a busy city. A more basic problem is fitting the entire structure into the frame. You can sometimes squeeze things in with a very wide angle lens (24 mm or wider), but you must often tip the camera up to include the tallest parts, which produces an effect called keystoning, in which the buildings appear to be falling backward.

The simplest cure for both problems is to move farther away and shoot with a normal or medium telephoto lens. Don't be afraid to include some of the building's surroundings if you must, even if they conflict with it philosophically: A modern shopping mall next to an ancient temple gives viewers a realistic perspective. Surroundings can even add to the beauty of the scene: Notre-Dame is frequently photographed reflecting in the Seine from far down the river.

As flash is fairly useless in very large spaces (and is prohibited in many religious buildings), you'll need to resort to a fast film (ISO 1000 or 1600) to photograph interiors, and even then a tripod will be necessary for exposures longer than about 1/30 second. Shoot from the ground up using a wide-angle lens to exaggerate the height of a massive nave; or climb to a balcony or choir loft to get a bird's-eye view of altars or stained glass windows (see page 14). A medium telephoto will enable you to isolate architectural details (see page 16) that you just can't get to physically.

Remember that these are houses of worship. Ask whether photography is permitted; if you're allowed to photograph, be discreet and *always* defer to those worshipping.

Focal Points

- **Shoot exteriors from nearby with a very wide-angle lens**
- **Move away and include surroundings**
- **Indoors, switch to a very fast film**

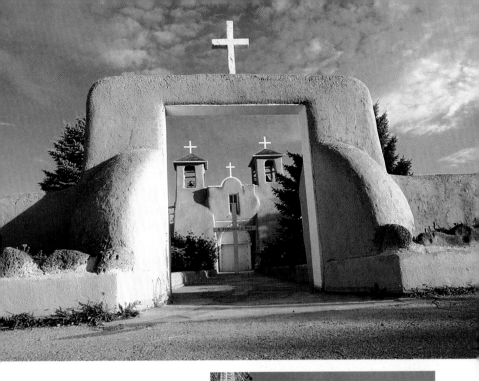

Stained Glass Windows

Stained glass windows can make wonderfully colorful and exotic pictures for your travel album—and they're simple to photograph. The nicest part is that, as with formal gardens, most of the creative work has been done for you by the glass artists.

Because you're shooting a translucent subject lit by the sun, you must pay attention to time of day and the intensity of sunlight. Bright but slightly overcast skies provide the best lighting and the most saturated colors. If the light is too harsh, the color and brightness range will be beyond the contrast range of the film.

Most automatic exposure systems do a good job of exposing for stained glass windows. The primary consideration is to read only the window and not the dark interior surroundings. If the window is big enough to fill the frame, just compose and shoot. If the window is smaller or farther away, switch to a spot-metering exposure mode in which the camera's exposure meter reads only a tiny area in the center of the frame. Alternatively, you can move physically closer to the window, take a reading when the window fills the frame, use your

exposure-lock feature to hold the setting, recompose to get the scene the way you want it, and shoot.

If your camera has an exposure-bracketing or -compensation feature, you can shoot additional exposures at one stop over and one stop under the recommended setting— especially if you're shooting slide film, which has much less exposure latitude than print film. If your point-and-shoot camera has a built-in flash that turns on automatically in dark settings, switch it off when you're shooting in a dark church interior. Flash bouncing off the glass will only create glare and diminish the intensity of the colors.

Don't be so wowed by the entire window that you ignore the myriad intricacies of color and shape that form the whole. Use a medium telephoto (85 mm) or telephoto zoom setting to isolate particularly arresting designs, or look for vignettes that capture the spiritual theme of the window.

14

Focal Points

- **Bright indirect sunlight yields saturated colors**
- **Expose for the glass not the surroundings**
- **Switch off flash to avoid glare**

Architectural Details

Snarling, sneering gargoyles, fancy stone filigree, rusting iron door knockers: Looking for eye-catching details in architecture can be fun when you're traveling, and capturing them on film can insert a whimsical theme into your photo album. Very often, too, the architectural style of a building is revealed in its smallest details: Elaborate wood fancywork

immediately betrays the Victorian period, just as splashy neon-and-glass shapes scream Art Deco.

One of the keys to capturing strong images of architectural detailing is tight composition. You must fill the frame to the brim (see page 108) with just your subject so there is no question about what you were photographing. If your subject is nearby, you can often isolate details with a normal lens or moderate telephoto. For more distant subjects—a stone griffin peering down from a bell tower, for instance—you'll need a long telephoto of around 200 mm.

Sometimes you can use a very long lens to compress several repeating details into a pattern (see page 120).

Pay particular attention to lighting as well. Light coming from the side is ideal because it provides the interplay of shadow and highlight that you need to give your subjects three-dimensional form and surface texture. If color is an important part of the composition (a pattern of mosaic tiles, for example), the soft, diffuse light of a hazy day will provide the most saturated hues.

The real secret to getting good detail shots, though, is simply becoming aware: pausing long enough to notice the myriad parts that make the whole. Cathedrals and palaces are probably the first subjects that come to mind when you're looking for details, but remember even a barn is rife with shapes and patterns when they are dramatized by good lighting and observed by a scrutinizing eye.

Focal Points

- **Move close to isolated details**
- **For distant vignettes, use a telephoto lens**
- **Use side light to accent form and texture**

In the Marketplace

Big city or small town, few corners of the world are without a thriving produce or arts-and-crafts market operating at least one day a week. In fact, in many rural places, the Saturday morning farmer's market is the highlight of weekly life. These markets offer prime opportunities to do some low-exertion photography—and have fun shopping at the same time.

I remember waking early one morning in a sleepy little Bavarian town to move my car (and avoid a parking ticket), only to poke my head out the door and find that the whole town had been transformed into a carnival-like flea market. Zowie! I risked the ticket and left the car where it was, to spend a wonderful day shopping and snapping.

If there's one thing you can count on in most markets, it's colorful displays of goods and colorful characters hawking them. Some markets—like the floating produce markets in Thailand, where women peddle their wares from boats—are so unusual that the most offhand snapshot can catch the exotic atmosphere. As markets (especially in warmer climates) generally open early in the day, you'll have to pull the covers off promptly to catch the peak activities,

but the gentle morning light will enhance the warmth of your pictures.

What to photograph? Color is everywhere, especially in a produce market, so look for interesting still lifes of exotic fruits and vegetables. Close-ups of individual artworks are great souvenirs, but I recommend buying something, too, if you want to make a new friend. Most people who sell their wares directly to the public are part huckster, so if you happen on a particularly gregarious one, snap a few quick portraits of him or her exhibiting a prize chicken or a one-of-a-kind piece of handicraft. If it's an open-air market, look for a high vantage point to get an overall shot as well.

Markets are crowded and almost everything photographs well with a wide-angle lens, so just bring the point-and-shoot even if you've got an SLR and lenses. A one-time-use panoramic (see page 44) is another good idea for sweeping street views. Above all, bring lots of film—and cash.

Focal Points

- **Get up early to catch the peak activity**
- **Search out colorful displays and colorful characters**
- **Don't scrimp on the film**

18

Friends' Faces

There's nothing wrong with taking lots of pictures of your friends or family posing rigid and glassy-eyed in front of every sign and historic marker you encounter, except that they'll all hate you for making them pose, and no one will want to look at the pictures later. Well, things may not get that drastic, but there are tricks that will make taking pictures of your travel companions more enjoyable for them and produce better pictures to boot.

One way to make your subjects look and act comfortable is to let them *be* comfortable. Rather than snapping them standing at attention in front of the Lincoln Memorial, let them sit on the steps chatting. Sitting or leaning on something gives people something to do with their arms and hands and makes them feel much less self-conscious. For variety, try to find poses where your subjects are looking at the scene around them, even if it means that they have their backs partially or even completely to the camera. You know who they are, they know who they are—what else matters?

If you insist on having your subjects face the camera, be sure that you're not asking them to squint straight into bright sunlight. Instead, try to find a spot of open shade, or alter your shooting position slightly so they're looking away from the sun. In any case, the faster you work—especially with kids—the more likely it is that your subjects will tolerate your forays into portraiture. Don't dally over camera controls. Compose the picture you want first, then have your subjects step into it.

Speaking of kids, you may want to abandon posing them altogether and wait until they're involved in some activity, like sloshing down a water slide or climbing up a sand dune. Keep shutter speeds at 1/250 second or faster to freeze action (see page 178), and shoot extra pictures to be sure of at least one clean shot.

Don't overlook ordinary moments either: sitting in a sidewalk café, gassing up the car, or just dozing by the hotel pool. Usually these are the times when everyone is most relaxed, and the pictures will reflect it.

Focal Points

- **Pose subjects informally to keep the mood relaxed**

- **Try to work in shady areas to avoid squints**

- **Let kids pick their own poses**

Strangers' Faces

For a lot of us, the very idea of walking up to strangers on the street and taking a picture of them is enough to bring on a cold sweat. But no other subject you will encounter will bring home the wonder and charm of far-flung places like portraits of the people who live there.

The best way to find interesting faces and characters is simply to wander where people gather: markets, fairs, city parks, and the like. In these situations, working candidly (that is, unobtrusively) is often your only alternative, as subjects come and go so quickly. A moderately long telephoto lens (my favorite is an 80 mm to 200 mm zoom) will enable you to remain at an inconspicuous distance, but remember there is a fine line between working politely from afar and appearing sneaky. If you are perceived as the latter, you will certainly draw more suspicion than cooperation. If you're spotted by your subject, simply smile and turn the camera away, or better yet, seize the opportunity to start a conversation in which you can ask him or her to pose.

Posing someone for a portrait isn't as mysterious or daunting as it sounds. Frame the scene tightly to take in just the head and shoulders, and try to keep direct eye contact with your subject. Don't automatically encourage people to smile: Allow them to be shy or pensive or curious. Portraits look best when the background is either simple or out of focus; one technique is to use a large aperture and selective focus (see page 168) to cast the background into a soft blur. Soft, even lighting is most flattering, so try also to pose your subject in the shade of a building or tree. Bright midday light from overhead is the worst; it will create strong shadows in the eye sockets (use flash fill—see page 154—to open them).

Finally, remember that there are places in the world where taking someone's picture is taboo. Ask at your hotel before you go out.

Focal Points

- **In crowds, work from a distance with a telephoto lens**
- **Try posing cooperative subjects**
- **Stick with gentle lighting—it's most flattering to faces**

Peter Guttman: Faces of the World

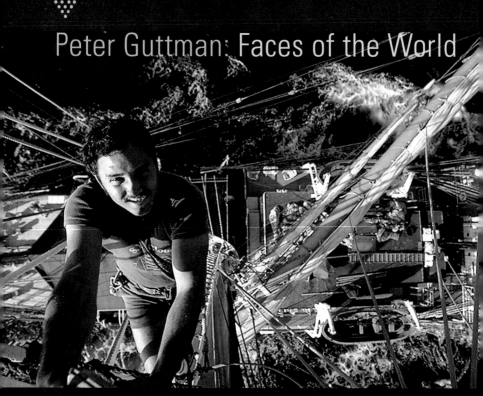

Peter Guttman is as much an adventurer as he is a photographer, and it is his thirst for new experiences—and new subjects to photograph—that drives his life. He has chased tornadoes, skydived, gone spelunking, ridden Olympic bobsleds, and climbed high into the rigging of tall ships and to the top of a radio tower at the North Pole. Guttman has had a lifelong passion for geography. In fact, it was discovering photography while working on his geography degree in college that set the seeds for his career. He spent a decade as a tour guide in North America—experience he credits with both expanding his geographic knowledge and giving him the opportunity to polish his photography skills. He has photographed in 140 countries and on assignment on all seven continents, and his work has been published in *Life, National Geographic* publications, *Vogue, The New York Times, Travel & Leisure,* and *Condé Nast Traveler.* Though he photographs all types of travel subjects, Guttman is particularly concerned with photographing people, especially primitive people: "I'm trying to record the purest unassimilated peoples on Earth, who are disappearing," he says. "We're moving very quickly toward homogenizing the planet." On these and the following pages are some of the faces and adventures he has preserved. He currently teaches a course in travel photography at the International Center of Photography in New York.

difficult existence as nomadic rein-
deer hunters. Both in clothing and in
face, the girl embodies the sense of
being guarded against the elements."

Muslim woman, Anjouan, Comoro
Islands. "This woman, in accordance
with Islamic law, was covering up—
by keeping her robe secured in her
mouth. She uses the clay-like mud
as a beauty treatment to keep her
skin moist in the heat of the sun. The
textures of the wall echo the textures on her face."

Feeding Pigeons, San Marco Plaza,
Venice. "His reactive pose seems to
mimic the hand gestures that are so
common in Italian conversation. He's
obviously getting more attention
than he bargained for."

Women, Cameron Highlands,
Malaysia. These are Muslim school-
girls coming from classes. What cap-
tivated me were those ovoid faces; I
tried to accentuate the shapes."

Melpa warriors, Western Highlands, Papua New Guinea (above). These people weren't discovered until the 1980s because of the rugged topography here. The face itself is a small vignette of the society, the culture, the landscape. The colors that are used to paint these warriors are natural pigments from bark, berries, and roots ."

Young girl, Mauritius (above). "I waited outside this Chinese shrine. . . . I asked her parents if I could pose her in front of it."

Beggar woman, Angkor Wat, Cambodia (left). Chiseled into the stone behind her are the Apsara—the dancing women. I only had about a minute and a half, but for me that's a long time to work with someone."

Cuna Indian, San Blas Islands, Panama (above). "I like to make the background or the setting of the people as vibrant and vivid as possible, letting it give some anthropological clue to their existence. These people are very creative, and that's what I wanted to show."

Sadhu, Jaipur, India (above). This holy man's body and personality and skin textures and hair are so wild to begin with that minimizing the background was the wisest thing to do."

Masai woman, manyatta compound, Kenya (left). "What particularly intrigued me was the anorexic stick-like appearance of her arm and how it resembled the wood framework of this mud and dung dwelling."

Iban man, Sarawak, Borneo (above). "This is one of the few shots where I used a flash; it was fairly deep inside a moist and dark rain forest and I was trying to illuminate the colored designs on his teeth."

Ndebele woman, South Africa (left). "This tribal group paint these extraordinary abstract designs on their dwellings. The woman is wearing a beaded wedding apron that seems to mirror some of the primary colors of the wall itself."

Ollantaytambo, Peru (above). In this valley, you visit people who are some of the purest genetic links to the Incans. This was taken near the market."

Tribal leader, Sulawesi, Indonesia (left). "I was impressed by the nobility and character in his face. In the background you can see his warrior shield. I used a 200 mm telephoto lens to enhance the composition."

Group Portraits

Anytime you try to pose more than three people in a photograph and catch them looking happy and relaxed, you'll understand why professional portrait photographers are so well paid. Photographing groups is not easy. But if you're traveling with a large family or group, or happen to encounter a crowd of friendly strangers, you'll need to confront the challenge.

Arranging a natural pose is the most awkward part of photographing a group, so try to be creative. Rather than lining them up in rows by height like your grammar school photographer did, clump them around a picnic bench, seat them on a grassy hillside, or just let them roost naturally, as the photographer did with the Chinese children at right.

Try to get everyone to lighten up: Better to capture a slightly disheveled-looking bunch who are enjoying themselves than to record them looking like a terrified gang facing a firing squad. Tell a joke (even if it's lame) or, if you're shooting travel companions, bring up a particularly silly event that happened during the trip. There's usually at least one live wire in every group, and a good way to get a funny picture is to put him or her in charge

of organizing the shot. If you can't get your crowd to strike a really at-ease pose, don't worry; standing around in a group in front of a camera *isn't* very natural. Get what you can and try again later.

Lighting in group portraits is important, because you want to be able to recognize people's faces. If possible, pose your group in a large area of open shade—under a tree or on the shaded steps of a hotel. If you're forced to work in harsh sunlight where shadows are obscuring faces, use the flash-fill mode (see page 154) of your built-in flash to open dark spots.

A wide-angle lens or wide zoom setting will obviously help you work closer and get more people into the frame, but be careful not to take in too much distracting background. If you're working with a really big group, consider taking a panoramic photograph (see page 44)—its unusual proportions will give a witty twist to the picture.

Focal Points
- **Keep the mood informal**
- **Use soft, diffuse lighting**
- **Try using a panoramic camera**

People at Work

Photographing people at work provides an intimate glimpse into what *real* life is like in different parts of the world. Often too, pictures of people at work identify destinations better than landmarks or scenery. Nothing describes life on Cape Cod better than a picture of a lobsterman unloading his day's catch, or identifies London like a shot of a bobby up to his neck in evening traffic.

While it's possible (and sometimes preferable) to photograph people at work candidly, it's usually better to ask their permission. Photographer Boyd Norton, who travels extensively around the world, says that asking your subjects about their work is an excellent way to build a photographic rapport: "Most people are proud of their accomplishments and soon lose themselves in talking about—and demonstrating—their skill. By then they've forgotten about your camera. . . ." Incidentally, Norton has learned to ask his subjects' permission in no less than eight languages—including Swahili and Navajo. Even if you don't speak the language, often a smile and a simple nod at your camera will get you permission.

One advantage of photographing people working is that you have built-in props. Holding a tool or a product makes people less self-conscious and solves the problem of what to do with their hands: A basket weaver can display a work in progress, for example. Use a normal lens to isolate your subject and the work, or if an interesting or exotic background warrants, use a wide-angle to include it as well; a telephoto will let you zoom in on a craftsperson's hands and tools.

Always work quickly and with a minimum of gear; even the friendliest of subjects will lose patience (and income) if you fuss too much with equipment. Also, unless you're desperate for light, try to shoot with the existing light—nothing kills spontaneity like the blast of an electronic flash. With fast films (ISO 400 or 1000), you can photograph people in surprisingly dim conditions—even by candlelight.

Focal Points

- **Capture destination-specific occupations**
- **Use tools for props**
- **Avoid flash if possible**

Sports

Sailing, skiing, rafting, baseball, soccer, golf, rock climbing—no matter where in the world you go, or when you go, sports are a part of daily life. The two major hurdles you have to overcome to photograph most sports are getting close to the action and stopping it.

Professional photographers rely on ultralong (and ultraexpensive) telephoto lenses (frequently 600 mm or longer) to capture such shots as an outfielder leaping over the center field wall. But often you can do with a little legwork and planning what expensive lenses do for pros. At a soccer match, for example, most of the action happens near the goal; stake your position there and you may even be able to shoot with just a normal or even a wide-angle lens. Some sports like track and field or ski racing also have finish lines that offer the combination of a good vantage point and high emotional impact.

While the goal in most sports photography is to isolate a particular player or action, when travel is involved it's just as important to provide the viewer with a sense of place: Where in the world is this sport being played? If you're photographing an informal cricket game among students at Oxford, including a Gothic dormitory in the background immediately helps place the photograph. A tight shot of a skier slicing down a snowy mountain could be taken almost anywhere, but include a chalet in the background and you instantly identify Switzerland.

The second obstacle, stopping action, depends on two things: a fast shutter speed (see page 162) and your directional relationship to the action. You can use a slower shutter speed to stop action that's moving directly toward or away from you than you can to stop action moving across your field of view. For example, you may be able to stop a race horse coming at you around the turn with a shutter speed of 1/125 second, but the same horse moving from left to right in front of you would require a speed of 1/1000 second or faster; use speeds somewhere in between if the horse is moving diagonally across your frame.

Focal Points

- **Fill the frame with action**
- **Include identifying background**
- **Use fast shutter speeds to stop action**

Silly Pictures

One quick trick for improving the pictures you take of your travel companions is this: Lighten up. Stop taking your pictures (and yourself) so seriously. Let silliness reign, and I guarantee your pictures will be more fun to look at and tons more fun to take. Allowing your subjects to slip into occasional fits of silliness may also keep them from plotting a mutiny against your camera mid-trip.

A few years ago I took a foot-long plastic lizard to Germany for three weeks (I also took a friend) and photographed it everywhere: in the airport, on the plane, in restaurants, and on the altar of the great cathedral (the Dom) in Cologne. My friend and I had a great time devising scenarios for photographing Lizzie, and some of our best pictures of the trip have a plastic lizard lurking in them. We got some strange looks from the Germans (I don't think they totally understood the concept), but we also had some great conversations with folks we probably wouldn't otherwise have met.

How to set your own silly streak in motion? Start by letting your subjects decide how *they* want to pose. Or give them a challenge: See if you can get the family to do a Rockettes kick on the beach or mimic holding the

Statue of Liberty's torch with an ice cream cone. Whatever the scene, be sure your subjects are in on the fun and that you're not catching them off-guard, or next time you may need to find someone else to hit the road with.

Focal Points

- **Look for or create light-hearted situations**
- **Don't be inhibited**
- **Try a funny prop**

Parades and Ceremonies

Because festivals, parades, and other ceremonies can infuse your travel photographs with a splash of color and excitement, they're worth making a special effort to take in. People tend to be less inhibited at such events, so your candid pictures of strangers will seem more friendly and intimate. As they usually celebrate something of historical, religious, or traditional significance, they can add depth to your travel album.

Some festivals—such as the annual running of the bulls in Pamplona, Spain—are annual highlights that draw crowds of tourists from around the world. Others may be less adventurous but can be equally chaotic both physically and visually. Finding a clear vantage point to shoot from, then, is vital. You can shoot from above, from a hotel balcony or a high set of steps, or you can arrive early and stake out a good shooting position before the hordes arrive. If you're unfamiliar with the event or its history, ask around a few days in advance; you may get ideas for where to position yourself.

What to shoot? People—especially children—are the heart of any special event, so use a zoom lens to isolate candid expressions and reactions in the participants and the crowds. Look also for costumes or decorations that symbolize the focus of the festivities—the American flag and Uncle Sam costumes are a colorful part of Fourth of July parades. What are the emblems of the event you're shooting? At religious ceremonies and events, take special care to avoid photographing any situations or scenes that are sacred to the participants.

Sometimes important ceremonies are held at night, presenting a real challenge in available-light photography. I was in the Dom Platz in Cologne, Germany, on the night when East and West Germany were reunited; lighting came from just a few broad floodlights. As the square was packed, my only option was to raise the camera over my head and take handheld exposures lasting several seconds. The images are blurred and full of motion, but they capture the excited and restless mood of the crowd.

Focal Points

- **Stake out a shooting spot early**
- **Show distinctive costumes**
- **Isolate crowd reactions**
- **Be flexible: content first, technique second**

Natural Places, Wild Faces

2

Landscape

In the hands of a creative photographer, an artful landscape can be made of any subject from a New England farm to an Inca ruin in Peru. Landscapes are simply photographs that describe an outdoor place—any place at all.

The natural inclination—especially in scenic areas—is to put on a wide-angle lens and randomly take in as much of a vista as possible, assuming that the beauty or intrigue of a place will carry the photograph. Usually it won't. While a wide-angle lens's ability to include a broad view can be a real blessing, often it is better to use a telephoto lens to isolate a particularly interesting portion of a scene. In either case, you must find a way to organize and present your landscapes with as little excess baggage as possible.

Try to think of a landscape photo as being like a short story that has a beginning (the foreground), a middle (the middle ground), and an ending (the background). In a farm scene, for example, you could use an old wagon as the foreground, a winding dirt road as the middle ground, and a bright red barn as the background. A farmer leading a horse up the road can stand in as your main character. (Scatter a few chickens around if you need some minor characters.) Very few landscapes will be so neatly arranged at first glance, so your main chore is finding a vantage point that translates to the viewer what it was that attracted your eye to the scene.

A landscape should also capture the spirit and mood of a place. Before you even raise a lens to the scene, pause to ask yourself what it is about it that appeals to you *emotionally.* Is it the yellow morning light glowing through the fields of hay? The color, direction, quality, and intensity of light (see Chapter 3) all have a profound effect on landscapes. Or is it the evening mist rising off the river? Weather in all its forms can work wonders with even the most common of scenes (see Chapter 3).

Focal Points

- **Isolate the essence of a place**
- **Tell a story**
- **Exploit mood, weather, and lighting**

There are times when recording a great, sweeping vista in its entirety is exactly what works best. Use a panoramic camera when it is the vastness or sweep of a scene that is its inherent power. Certain subjects lend themselves naturally: bridges, covered bridges, seascapes, city skylines, and large groups of people.

There are special cameras designed just for taking panoramic pictures. True professional panoramic cameras use a pivoting lens that sweeps across a curved film plane to create very, very wide views, up to a full circle of 360 degrees. The bad news here is that they're expensive (from $1,500 to $25,000); the good news is that there are cheaper alternatives

44

that produce quite acceptable results.

These pseudopanoramics incorporate a wide-angle lens combined with a mask over the film plane that blocks off the top and bottom of the frame, in effect creating elongated panoramic-like pictures. Some cameras allow you to change to the panorama mode at the flip of a switch mid-roll; others require that you physically insert a mask before loading the film (which means you have to shoot the whole roll in panoramic format). Also commonly available are one-time-use panoramic specialty cameras that have built-in masks.

Though neither type of camera is

truly panoramic, when the pictures are printed in panoramic format (usually 3½ x 10 inches), the wide-view effect can be stunning. The film does require special printing, so be sure to tell your lab that your film includes panoramic images.

Taking panoramic images isn't any more difficult than normal photography. Because you are taking very wide pictures, watch the edges of the viewfinder to be sure that you're including only what you truly want. It's important to keep the horizon level and near the middle of the frame; otherwise the horizon line will bend—upward if the horizon is too low or downward if the horizon is too high.

Focal Points

- **Use panoramic cameras for sweeping vistas**

- **Don't restrict yourself to horizontal shots**

- **Keep the horizon level**

Panorama: Assemblage

An even more inventive way to create panoramic images is to stand in one place with a conventional camera and take several pictures of a scene while rotating your head (and the camera) between each successive exposure. You can then piece the finished prints into a kind of panoramic collage. Henry Fox Talbot, one of photography's pioneers, experimented with the technique as early as 1843—only four years after the invention of photography.

The technique works best if you keep the camera mounted on a tripod so that each successive exposure is level with the others. Unlike shooting with panoramic cameras, which rely on wide-angle lenses, this method works best with normal or mild telephoto lenses. You can take anywhere from two to a dozen or more images; the total angle of view is limited only by the number of pictures you take and the angle of view of the lens.

In composing the scene, be sure that you overlap each shot slightly (about 10 to 20 percent), so you have an easier time matching them up later. Use a specific landmark—a tree or the edge of a building—as a reference mark for setting up the next shot: If you have a pine tree on the far right of the first exposure, use that same tree at the left edge of the next frame. If you want to make things more creative, you might even try mixing horizontals and verticals in the same assemblage or changing lenses between shots.

Try also to maintain an even level of exposure throughout the entire sequence of pictures. In photographing the assemblage of the river above, for example, I took readings from the autumn foliage and used that exposure for all four shots. While this caused the dimmer left and right edges to fall into blackness, it kept the tonalities in the foliage and water relatively consistent from print to print. Shoot color print film (as opposed to slide film) so that, if necessary, you can have prints color matched during the printing stage.

Unless you have an uncontrollably compulsive personality, don't worry about being too precise in assembling the final images. For artistic and other reasons (like keeping your sanity), I recommend

being a little more free-spirited about it. Match the prints as closely as possible, but overlap them if you have to and don't try for flawless edges. The overall effect is what you're after, and artistic license forgives slight errors.

Focal Points

- **Use a wide-angle or normal lens**
- **Let edges of pictures overlap**
- **Keep exposure even**
- **Use a tripod**

Mountain Scenery: Scale

Friends of mine—just casual shooters—returned from the Canadian Rockies with stacks of photos. The areas around Banff and Lake Louise, in particular, excited them so much that they shot double the number of pictures they had on previous vacations. Their enthusiasm waned when they discovered that, in many shots, the majesty of the mountains had evaporated in the translation to film. One picture that included a distant group of hikers on a glacier, however, really nailed the Rockies' scope and grandeur.

My friends learned an important lesson about photographing mountains: You must include some visual clue to indicate the true magnitude of the scene around you. Scale (see page 130) is probably more important in shooting mountain peaks and ranges than with any other subject.

One way to establish a sense of scale is to use a wide-angle lens (24 mm to 35 mm) or wide-zoom setting and include an immediate foreground subject—a clump of wildflowers or a travel companion, for example. Putting close foreground subjects into the scene helps heighten the feeling of "presence" in mountain landscapes, but the downside is that wide-angle shots often make the mountains appear to diminish rather than increase in size.

To make the mountains look more imposing, use a moderate telephoto and include a middle-ground subject for scale, such as a single pine tree or a barn. A telephoto lens will compress the space between foreground or middle ground and background and enhance the apparent size of the mountains. Using a telephoto lens also exaggerates the effects of a naturally occurring phenomenon known as aerial perspective. This effect occurs when atmospheric haze makes each layer of progressively distant peaks appear lighter in tone and color. The diminishing density is perceived by the eye as distance—thus further exaggerating the scale of the scene.

Focal Points

- **Include objects of known size**
- **Frame distant peaks with nearby objects**
- **Compress space with long lenses**

Mountain Scenery: Lighting

The best mountain photos are made by photographers who rise before the sun and rest only after it has. In his book *Mountain Light,* celebrated mountaineer and outdoor photographer Galen Rowell writes that "light during the magic hours [dusk and dawn] mixes in endless combinations, as if someone in the sky were shaking a kaleidoscope." The pinks, yellows, golds, and reds of dusk and dawn are hallmarks of his work and make Rowell's shots instantly recognizable.

At very high altitudes, just before sunrise or after sunset, nature may also reward your dedication with a very special phenomenon called alpenglow. This brilliant crimson glow emerges when blue light is scattered by the atmosphere and a predominance of red light briefly ignites peaks in warm, radiant hues. Alpenglow often illuminates the clouds around mountain peaks as well.

In addition to the continuous color changes, the raking light of dusk and dawn imparts texture, depth, and three-dimensional form to photos of mountains. Immediately before or after a storm are also great times to go picture-hunting. Many of Ansel Adams's most famous portraits of

Yosemite's peaks were made in the gathering or departing turmoil of a storm. Try to anticipate scenes where peaks disappear in descending gloom or shafts of sunlight burst through dissipating cloud banks.

One problem you will encounter at high altitudes is an excess of ultraviolet light, which results in atmospheric haze. As I've mentioned, you can use this haze to advantage, but if it is obscuring your subject, you may need to place a filter over your SLR lens. A UV or strong skylight filter (81B or 81C) will absorb some of this excess, but a polarizing filter (see page 176) is perhaps the most effective tool.

Exposure in mountain regions can be tricky because excessive light reflecting from haze, mist, or snowfields can trick the meter into underexposure. When you suspect conditions may be fooling your meter, set your exposure-compensation dial to overexpose the scene by a full stop or bracket in full stops.

Focal Points

- **Shoot early or late; avoid midday**
- **Watch for dramatic color events**
- **Use exposure compensation**

Mountain Scenery: Lighting

The best mountain photos are made by photographers who rise before the sun and rest only after it has. In his book *Mountain Light,* celebrated mountaineer and outdoor photographer Galen Rowell writes that "light during the magic hours [dusk and dawn] mixes in endless combinations, as if someone in the sky were shaking a kaleidoscope." The pinks, yellows, golds, and reds of dusk and dawn are hallmarks of his work and make Rowell's shots instantly recognizable.

At very high altitudes, just before sunrise or after sunset, nature may also reward your dedication with a very special phenomenon called alpenglow. This brilliant crimson glow emerges when blue light is scattered by the atmosphere and a predominance of red light briefly ignites peaks in warm, radiant hues. Alpenglow often illuminates the clouds around mountain peaks as well.

In addition to the continuous color changes, the raking light of dusk and dawn imparts texture, depth, and three-dimensional form to photos of mountains. Immediately before or after a storm are also great times to go picture-hunting. Many of Ansel Adams's most famous portraits of Yosemite's peaks were made in the gathering or departing turmoil of a storm. Try to anticipate scenes where peaks disappear in descending gloom or shafts of sunlight burst through dissipating cloud banks.

One problem you will encounter at high altitudes is an excess of ultraviolet light, which results in atmospheric haze. As I've mentioned, you can use this haze to advantage, but if it is obscuring your subject, you may need to place a filter over your SLR lens. A UV or strong skylight filter (81B or 81C) will absorb some of this excess, but a polarizing filter (see page 176) is perhaps the most effective tool.

Exposure in mountain regions can be tricky because excessive light reflecting from haze, mist, or snowfields can trick the meter into underexposure. When you suspect conditions may be fooling your meter, set your exposure-compensation dial to overexpose the scene by a full stop or bracket in full stops.

Focal Points

- **Shoot early or late; avoid midday**
- **Watch for dramatic color events**
- **Use exposure compensation**

Tropical Beaches

The glistening white sands, turquoise waters, and vibrant blue skies of tropical beaches are the stuff of which wall calendars (and daydreams) are made. Capturing the simple beauty of such scenes is relatively easy if you keep a few basic concepts in mind.

Because tropical beaches have such inherent prettiness, finding attractive compositions isn't hard. For broad views, use a wide-angle lens and look for vantage points where the curving line of the sea lures the eye into the scene—perhaps leading to a particularly attractive palm grove or a row of beached sailboats. In places like the Caribbean or the South Pacific, where the sea and hillsides are close neighbors, climbing to a clearing and shooting down at the beach below may reveal vistas unseen from sea level. Be sure to use a small aperture (or your Landscape exposure mode), so everything is in focus from near to far. Don't be afraid to let your designs border on abstraction; sometimes simple arrangements of sand, sea, and sky are the most effective.

Including people, as in the shot at right, provides a good center of interest and also helps establish scale, but take care with exposure. Tropical beaches are very bright and contrasty, and the intense light reflecting off the sand will fool your camera into turning the sugar-white sands gray and casting your human subjects into silhouette (see page 166). One compromise if you have an SLR or a sophisticated point-and-shoot is to use your camera's exposure-compensation feature to add a full stop of exposure to the suggested settings.

Better still, try working early and late in the day, when the light is less harsh and contrast isn't such a problem. The low angle of the sun at these times also casts long shadows that give scenes a sense of depth and three-dimensional relief. If you are forced to work at midday, be sure to use film with a speed of ISO 100 or slower, so you are not working beyond your camera's available range of shutter speed and aperture combinations (see page 164).

Focal Points
- **Capture expansive views**
- **Don't let bright sand fool your meter**
- **Include people**

Rocky Shorelines

The rocky shores of Maine or Scandinavia or the southwest coasts of England and Ireland provide a study in the absolute power and relentless energy of the sea. The best time to photograph the clash between surf and shore is at high tide, especially just prior to or after a storm or a full moon, when the sea is at its most volatile. Rather than try to capture the entire shore, use the longest lens you have, preferably in the 200 mm to 300 mm range, to isolate a single wave as it explodes onto a shapely rock formation. A fast shutter speed (1/250 second or faster) will freeze the spray, but timing is critical: You must fire the shutter an instant *before* the wave makes contact to catch it at its explosive peak. Use your autowind or motor drive to fire off three or four successive shots to increase your odds of getting a winner.

In calmer weather, you can use a wide-angle lens to capture a striking arrangement of rocks as the seas gently envelop them. Even in these gentler situations, timing is crucial. In his book *Examples: The Making of 40 Photographs,* Ansel Adams writes: "Surf is seldom predictable; in its ebb and flow it constantly presents fresh shapes, and the eye must be swift and anticipation keen to expose at the most favorable moment. . . ." Brief exposures (1/125 second or faster) will snare the shapes and patterns of the advancing or receding sea, while very long exposures (from 1/4 to several seconds with a tripod) will paint the shore and rocks with an impressionistic glossy sheen.

Don't overlook the world at your feet: the little tidal pools where starfish and crabs and seaweed present a miniature diorama of sea life. A polarizing filter (see page 176) will help you remove surface reflections and see deeper into the pools.

In any shoreline situation, remember that sand and salt and cameras don't mix. On windy days, or when there is a heavy spray from the surf, keep your gear in a plastic pack and remove it only for shooting. Always load and unload your camera in a protected place, away from the hazards of water and sand.

Focal Points

- **Vary shutter speeds to freeze or blur wave action**
- **Don't overlook sea life in tidal pools**
- **Protect your gear from sand and sea**

In the Desert

Hostile and uninviting though they may seem, deserts can be wonderfully rewarding for photographers. We tend to visualize deserts as vast, arid wastelands, but in fact, most are rich with life.

In the more barren desert regions, because the geologic and graphic components are so minimal—sand, rock, sky, and some plants—your compositions will by necessity often verge on the stark and abstract. In searching for and composing such scenes, then, exploit the visual simplicity to reveal the harsh nature of the place: ripples of wind-driven sand cresting into nomadic dunes, fractured patterns of cracking mud in long-dry watering holes, the delicate trail of lizard tracks leading from rock to rock. Textures (see page 122) abound here too, and you can really pop them out with low-angle light from the side or rear.

In regions that get some water, the shapes and textures of tenacious forms of plant life may be the main attraction. In the saguaro forests of southern Arizona, for instance, the fanciful profiles of the giant cacti make dramatic silhouettes against a sunset sky. In spring, especially after a wet winter, the desert floor often erupts into a tapestry of colorful blooms. Planning your visit for peak blooming periods requires research and sometimes flexibility, but the satisfaction is worth it.

Whatever the specific environment, take to heart all the cautions you've heard about deserts: Heat, nasty insects, sharp cactus spines, and rough footing can be torture if you're not prepared for them. Once, in the desert outside Phoenix, I became so enamored of the little lizards that lived under plants that I began kicking at scrub brush to drive them out. Only after several minutes did it occur to me that the places where I was sticking my foot were probably as appealing to rattlesnakes as they were to lizards.

The desert heat can be brutal at midday, and the light is not attractive; save your film for the low-angle light of early morning and late afternoon. Always, but always, bring more water and film than you think you'll need. Store both in a white cooler on the floor of the car.

Focal Points

- **Look for shapes and textures**
- **Try visiting during peak bloom periods**
- **Don't forget safety**

Canyons

For me, there is no place as mysterious or haunting as the canyons and valleys of the American Southwest. Driving or hiking through them is like looking into the face of the history of the planet and of the people who first inhabited it. Translating these transcendent images onto a tiny piece of film is no mean feat, but it is a worthwhile challenge.

Because most canyon regions are vast in scale, I always have mixed emotions about wanting to see *all* of a place at once while simultaneously wanting to linger and study its infinitely curious details. The first time I visited the Valley of Fire State Park, north of Las Vegas, I got so involved in photographing a set of rock formations called the Beehives that before I knew it, the sun was setting and I'd seen only a fraction of the park.

It's best to read about an area and, if possible, do an overall tour before you start shooting. Then, narrow down a shooting plan to a few specific ideas. For instance, there is usually one type of geographic feature that typifies a particular region: the great stone arches of

Utah, the ancient cliff dwellings of Mesa Verde in Colorado, or, of course, the unfathomable vastness of the Grand Canyon. Focusing on one aspect of the whole helps to fight off the temptation (and frustration) of trying to capture everything you see.

Once you've decided on a particular geologic focus, try to match it to a specific design technique (see pages 104–137). In Bryce Canyon in Utah, for example, you would certainly want to concentrate on the shapes of the stone spires by silhouetting them against an open sky or finding patterns in the repeating shapes. At the Grand Canyon, you would want to find ways to establish size (see page 130).

Don't ignore the human history of the canyons you visit, either. Whether it's a shot of a rock painting or a Navajo herdsman at work, reminders of human history will round out your scenic album nicely.

Focal Points

- **Research the natural and social history of a locale**
- **Focus on a theme or geologic feature**
- **Budget your shooting time**

Wild tropical environments elicit a deep sense of mystery and adventure in most of us. Resist the temptation to climb to a clearing to capture as broad a view as possible; all you're likely to get is a vague green mass with little detail or sense of scale.

Instead, search out the myriad visual vignettes that impart your excitement: a colorful burst of jungle flower, a graphic spray of giant ferns, or a waterfall surging through dense vegetation. Forest wildlife (see photographer Boyd Norton's essay beginning on page 76), though elusive, is ever present; tour guides can often help you spot birds or snakes, but you'll need a fairly long lens (135 mm to 200 mm) to get close views.

Lighting in these environments presents a twofold problem: The canopy of treetops makes it dim, and it is almost always dappled and contrasty. A tripod and/or fast film will help you deal with the former, but contrast will still bring exposure problems. For close-up subjects, using flash fill (see page 54) will lessen contrast. For wider views, try using the contrasting tones as part of your compositions: Convert the clash of light and shadow into graphic designs.

A more pragmatic problem is protecting your gear (and yourself) from the onslaught of humidity and moisture. Modern cameras are full of and totally dependent on thousands of tiny electrical circuits that are susceptible to too much moisture. A photographer friend of mine on assignment in Jamaica recently had to switch to a manual camera when moisture kept interfering with the light readings on his two electronic SLRs. Keep your cameras packed in self-locking plastic bags that contain a large supply of desiccant (silica gel packets are available at most camera shops). As film is equally susceptible to heat and humidity, store it in and return it immediately to the vapor-proof plastic canister it comes in. Finally, be sure to bring rain gear, rubber hiking boots, and an umbrella—you'd be surprised how many people don't!

Focal Points

- **Go for mystique with close-ups and details shots**
- **Battle low light with fast films and camera supports**
- **Protect cameras and film from moisture and humidity**

Rivers and Waterfalls

Whether you're trekking through wilderness or simply strolling in the countryside, an especially pretty river or waterfall is a visual treat. There is something appealing and refreshing about the perpetual motion of water that translates readily to film.

One way to capture the rush and tumble of moving water is by using a slow shutter speed and letting the water blur into shiny white, streaming ribbons. You often see the technique used in advertising and greeting-card shots, and it's easy to duplicate if you own an SLR that lets you choose your own shutter speed.

Start by loading your camera with a slow-speed (ISO 64 or 25) film and setting it on a sturdy tripod. The trick is to set a shutter speed slow enough that the water moves through the frame while the shutter is open. The exact shutter speed will depend on the speed of the water and the degree of blur you're after. With a fast-moving stream or waterfall or where you just want a hint of a blur, you can use speeds as fast as 1/15 second; with slower-moving streams or to let the ribbons of water appear to be passing entirely through the frame, use a shutter speed of a full second or longer. If the light is bright, you may have to put a neutral-density

filter (see page 174) over the lens to cut down on the light so you can use such long exposures.

And if you don't own an adjustable camera? You can sometimes trick the camera into selecting a slow shutter speed by simply loading it with very slow (ISO 25) film and working when the light is relatively dim. You'll still need use a tripod, though, to keep everything other than the water steady.

Of course, you can also use fast shutter speeds to halt the motion of water. This method can be very effective with particularly tumultuous falls or rivers.

You can add power to compositions like these by finding low vantage points so the water looks like it's going to gush right out of the print. Don't ignore rivers and falls in winter, when freezing temperatures turn swirling flows into fantastic frozen shapes.

Focal Points

- **Use slow film and long shutter speeds to blur water**
- **When needed, use a neutral-density filter over the lens**
- **Shoot from water level to heighten drama**

Autumn Colors

Autumn foliage always reminds me of a long, slow-burning fireworks display. It begins by sparking a few leaves or a branch, ignites entire trees into brilliant red-orange embers, and then finally explodes the entire countryside into a flaming finale of color.

To enjoy photographing the colors, just show up on time. Where I live in Connecticut, the whole spectacle, start to finish, lasts about three or four weeks, but the peak lasts only a few days. Vermonters I've spoken with tell you that they can spot the peak *hour* of color! If you're traveling to New England or any other region specifically to shoot the autumn colors, it's a good idea to give yourself a spread of several days. Be sure to call tourist offices or the local chamber of commerce in advance—many have recorded leaf-peepers' updates.

Autumn foliage is one of the few subjects that can make even the most casual snapshot attractive. To extract its essence, though, takes some thought. Most important, try not to be so overwhelmed by the glory of it all that you miss the leaves for the trees or the trees for the forest. In his handsome book *The View from the Kingdom,* which

documents life in the northeast corner of Vermont, photographer Richard Brown illustrates autumn with eloquent pictures that range from rambling, mist-filled vistas to giant maples aglow in a sheep meadow to close-ups of fallen leaves beaded with rain.

Whatever the specific subject, pay particular attention to lighting. Because the colors are so brilliant themselves, they photograph well in a variety of lighting conditions. On sunny days work early and late, when the sun, backlighting the leaves, creates a translucent glow. Cloudy days can be good, too, because they tend to create a muted but very earthy spectrum of colors. Avoid including too much gray sky, which will just appear as blank space in a print. After a gentle rain, when the colors are intensely saturated, you can use a polarizing filter (see page 176) to remove surface reflections for even richer color, as well as to deepen the blue of a clearing sky.

Focal Points

- **Plan trips for peak foliage periods**
- **Mix wide and close views for visual variety**
- **Use lighting that accents colors or creates moods**

Moonlit Landscapes

Opportunities for shooting a landscape by moonlight don't present themselves every night when you're traveling, but when they do, it's nice to know how to capture them. You can take two types of moonscapes: those that feature the moon itself (usually a full moon) in the frame and those that are simply landscapes exposed by the light of the moon.

The former are the simplest and are best made shortly after the sun has set, just as the moon is beginning to rise: The moon appears largest at this time because of the land reference of the horizon and the refraction of the earth's atmosphere. As lighting is predominantly from the twilit sky, you'll still get a sufficient amount of foreground detail. Look for a simple scene that you can compose with a telephoto lens 300 mm or longer; remember that the longer the lens, the larger the moon will appear. If you are using color negative film, take a meter reading of the scene and shoot. When you're shooting slide film, bracket your exposures (see page 164) by a full stop, both under and over the suggested reading. Be careful to avoid exposures of more than a few seconds, or the moon's shape will become elongated.

If your camera allows you to make exposures of several seconds or longer, landscapes illuminated exclusively by the full moon but not including the moon can make eerie, ethereal pictures. The technique works best with snowscapes or beaches, because light reflected from snow or sand brightens the entire scene. Exposures will still be quite long; with ISO 400 film, start with two seconds at *f*/2.8 and then make several additional exposures, doubling the time for each successive shot. You'll need a tripod.

If you want to be really creative, consider taking a double exposure (see page 184). The simplest method is to make one exposure of just the moon using a very long lens (300 mm or longer) and another of an interesting landscape, then combine them later in a slide duplicator.

Focal Points

- **Include the mood or use only its illumination**

- **Exaggerate the moon's relative size with long telephoto lenses**

- **Expose landscapes several seconds or longer**

Close-Ups

The world is full of tiny things that can draw a curious eye. Often seemingly insignificant details tell the story of a locale as well as broad views do. In a slide show, a close-up of a painted Chinese character is the perfect sequel to a Beijing street view.

The degree of closeness you can achieve will depend largely on your camera. Most point-and-shoot cameras have a minimum focusing distance of around 1½ to 2 feet. Some zoom-lens-type point-and-shoots have a macro (close-up) mode that enables you to work much closer—often as close as a few inches (a feature worth considering if small subjects excite you). In either case, you'll know when you're trying to take a picture that's beyond the camera's close-focus capability, because the autofocus won't lock on. With most cameras the correct-focus indicator light will blink rapidly and the shutter release won't fire. All you can do is back off and recompose at a greater distance.

With an SLR camera, on the other hand, the degree of closeness is almost unlimited. A variety of accessories can be used to provide ever-increasing magnification. If you take close-ups only occasionally, a simple set of screw-on close-up filters will provide an inexpensive solution. For more serious work, a macro lens or a zoom with a macro feature offers superior quality.

Whatever camera equipment you have, using a fast (ISO 400) film is very important: The closer you get, the less depth of field there is (see page 168) and the more camera shake is magnified. Fast films allow higher shutter speeds and smaller apertures, which help correct both problems.

The secret to close-ups is just seeing, being aware. I often go shooting with a friend who finds close-up subjects in all the places where I see only wide expanses. I'll be photographing the sweep of a Cape Cod beach, and she'll discover the colors in a starfish clinging to a rock.

Focal Points

- **Look for interesting details**
- **Use macro lenses or close-up filters**
- **Minimize camera shake with fast films and high shutter speeds**

Under the Sea

Other than a few special pieces of gear and some unique shooting conditions that you must be aware of, taking pictures at depths of up to 12 feet is relatively straightforward and requires a minimal investment.

First, you'll need a camera that's safe underwater or a way to keep your terrestrial camera dry while it's submerged. For occasional underwater photography—such as a once-a-year island vacation—one-time-use underwater cameras will let you take pictures down to a depth of 12 feet. They come preloaded with color film, so you can just plunge in and shoot. Several brands of reloadable underwater cameras are also available, ranging from fixed-focus point-and-shoots to sophisticated SLRs. (Check diving magazines for ads or reviews.)

You can adapt your terrestrial camera for down-under shooting using an underwater housing. Inexpensive plastic-bag-type housings (safe to depths of about 100 feet with an SLR) are available for point-and-shoot, SLR, and some video cameras. They feature a built-in glove that allows you to manipulate camera controls under water and glass windows for the lens and the viewfinder. For deeper dives, a rigid

acrylic housing will provide ultimate protection to your camera.

Whatever the camera, getting good results underwater requires attention to the nature of the environment. Even very clear water acts as a filter, absorbing both light and color (especially red), so it's important to use a moderately fast (ISO 200) film. Colors will photograph naturally to a depth of about 10 feet but fade away quickly beyond that. Using either a built-in or a detachable accessory flash will restore colors and is the best method for providing consistent lighting, especially with close-ups. Below a depth of 12 feet, a flash is a necessity.

The real keys to success are patience and practice. Fish and other sea creatures have busy agendas that don't include posing for you; if you find waiting for them frustrating, practice on more stationary subjects like colorful anemones and corals.

Focal Points

- **Use underwater cameras or special housings**
- **Stay within 10 feet of the surface for the best colors**
- **Use flash to restore color at greater depths**

Caves and Caverns

Caves and caverns, from the more famous tourist sites to the uncharted gems discovered while adventuring, will put your existing-light photographic skills to the ultimate test.

In theatrically lighted tourist caves, such as the Carlsbad Caverns National Park in New Mexico, the light is relatively dim and the spaces are vast. Flash is useless except for close-ups of stalagmites and stalactites. Even if the flash is powerful enough for wider shots, it only washes away the colorful artificial lighting. Tripods are usually not allowed; instead, you'll be forced to resort to a very fast (ISO 1000 or 1600) film so you can get sharp pictures with your handheld camera. It pays to chat up rangers or tour guides in these places, too: On slow days or in the off-season they may be willing to give you private tours at a pace that allows the use of a tripod.

Spelunking, the sport of cave exploring, is a way to find caves and

caverns that no tour group will ever see or photograph, but it is dangerous and physically demanding. It can be done only in the company of experienced cavers—never venture into any cave alone—and the photographic equipment you carry will have to be secondary to necessary climbing supplies.

In wild caves, one trick for lighting a large area is to place your camera on a tripod with the shutter locked open in the B position and then fire your flash multiple times to paint the room with light. The method requires experimenting, but you can use it to light any size space.

Tourist cave or lost cavern, however, you must take care to protect your camera from high levels of dust and humidity and from hard knocks. Store cameras and lenses in padded cases and, in very damp environments, in locking plastic bags or even underwater housings. Be sure, too, that the front lens element or filter is kept clean.

Focal Points

- **Shoot with ISO 1000+ films**
- **Use existing light in tourist caves**
- **Paint with flash in wilderness caves**

Animals on Their Own

Getting good pictures of domestic animals is easy; getting good shots of wildlife is not. I always find it comforting to encounter the familiar faces of cats and dogs and farm animals in foreign lands. The key to making pictures of them interesting as travel photos is to back away a bit and show the animal in the context of its locale: the dog snoozing on the Greek sidewalk at right, or a cow grazing in the meadow of a French château. Beasts of burden around the world—camels in the Middle East, llamas in South America, water buffalo in Asia—make fascinating pictures, too.

The ultimate challenge in animal photography is photographing creatures on their own terms: in the wild. Getting good wildlife pictures is a very special skill that many photographers—including Boyd Norton, whose superb portfolio of wildlife images begins on page 76—devote much of their lives to mastering.

The chief obstacle is getting close enough to the animals to take recognizable and dramatic pictures. Long lenses, especially those in the 300 mm to 600 mm range, will certainly help, but assuming that owning one will guarantee you exciting pictures is like believing that buying a great saxophone will make you play like John Coltrane. The real tools aren't physical but mental: patience, planning, and a deep knowledge of the habits of the animals you're pursuing. If you're on a photographic safari or wildlife photo tour, your guide can help, but preparing in advance by reading about or watching videos on the indigenous wildlife of your destination will give you a significant advantage.

In such popular wildlife sanctuaries as Yellowstone National Park in Wyoming, animals are abundant and accustomed to human visitors; in others, shooting platforms may have been set up to let photographers get close to animals. Whatever the situation, be ready. To come within shooting distance of an animal and lose the photo because you have to reload your camera can put a major dent in the thrill of the experience.

Focal Points

- **Show domestic and work animals in their everyday settings**
- **To photograph wildlife, research habits and habitats**
- **Be sure your camera is always ready to shoot**

Boyd Norton: Wild Creatures

Photographer and writer Boyd Norton has spent the past 25 years documenting the ever-diminishing wild places and exotic creatures of the world. From Komodo "dragons" in Indonesia to grizzly bears in Alaska to zebras and lions on the veld of Africa, there are few wild environments or animals that he has not encountered. Photography is actually Norton's second career; his first was as a nuclear physicist in the 1960s. It was during this time that he became involved with environmental causes (he was among the small band of environmentalists who halted the damming of the Snake River at Hell's Canyon in Idaho) and soon turned to the camera as a means to reveal the beauty—and fragility—of the wilderness.

He devoted himself to photography full-time in 1970, and since then, his photo essays and articles have appeared in *Time, National Geographic, Smithsonian, Audubon, Condé Nast Traveler, Stern,* and *Vogue.* He has also published a dozen books, two of which, *The African Elephant: Last Days of Eden* and *The Mountain Gorilla,* are classics in wildlife photography and literature. Among his other books are *Baikal: Sacred Sea of Siberia* (with Peter Matthiessen), *Divided Twins: Alaska and Siberia* (with Yevgeny Yevtushenko), and *Boyd Norton's Outdoor Photography.* He teaches photographic workshops in the United States, Africa, and Asia, and between adventures he lives in Evergreen, Colorado.

Hippos, Tanzania.
"You have to know that things like this are likely to happen and pay attention to what they're doing. I noticed that one hippo was moving closer to another and I was anticipating that the second might object."

Cheetahs, Kenya (opposite).
"To get good wildlife photographs you really have to exercise a lot of patience."

Grizzly bear and cubs, Alaska. "When another bear started moving upstream toward the family, I focused on these guys because I knew they would focus on that bear."

Wolverine, Alaska. "I've talked to people who have lived in Alaska for 30 years and never even seen one.... I was prepared when it came to within 30 feet of us, so close that the big telephoto was useless; I used my second camera with a 70 to 200 mm zoom."

Mountain gorilla, Rwanda. "It's the kind of shot that is borderline clutter, but it's clutter with a purpose. It helps to convey a sense of the habitat of the mountain gorilla—very thick, high-altitude rain forest."

Mountain goats, Colorado . "These animals are fairly tolerant of people, but you can't pressure them too much. I just waited for a half hour or so until they moved onto these rocks above me. All I did was whistle once and they looked up at me."

Lions, Kenya (left).

Starling, Kenya (below). "I was watching an acacia tree about 8 or 10 feet away as this starling kept landing on this one branch, swooping around, and landing back in the same spot. I set up the camera on the tripod, and when it landed, shot its picture."

Zebra, Kenya (opposite). "I had motor drive on. I panned with the action and burned up a whole roll of film on that one zebra; this is the only picture that came out. The problem is that you never quite know what you're going to get."

Sibling elephants, Kenya (left). "I was with the herd for maybe two or three hours. As these two walked up to each other, I sensed that this was a good photo-op, so I prepared and shot."

Lions, Kenya (below). "I call this environmental photography; it conveys the sense of what lions are like; their color blends in with the color of the grasses; they're predators lying in wait."

Four sea lions, Galápagos (opposite). "This is a reflection of how tolerant the animal life of Galapagos is of humans: When I was taking this shot, I backed up and nearly fell over one; he kind of barked at me, like, 'Get out of here.'"

Zoos and Aquariums

It may not be quite as thrilling to photograph a lion or a zebra in a zoo as it is in the veld of Africa, but you can still make some terrific pictures. Because you can get much closer to your quarry, you can work with shorter lenses. While you might need a 400 mm or 600 mm telephoto to bring a lion or a polar bear up close in the wild, in a zoo you can get similar shots with lenses in the 180 mm to 300 mm range, or shorter. With smaller animals and reptiles that are behind wire or in glass enclosures, you can even work with macro lenses. I've photographed deadly snakes at New York's Bronx Zoo from just inches away.

In composing pictures of captive animals, I like to shoot some images that disguise the captive aspect and others that exploit it. To keep the human environment from showing, look for vantage points that hide fences or other barriers. You can make wire fencing or bars seem to disappear by working close to them with a long telephoto and using a wide aperture for shallow depth of field; be sure the autofocus frame (see page 161) is on the subject and not the bars. Conversely, if you want to make a statement about the plight of animals in captivity, look for shots that emphasize the confinement: a

leopard peering out from between steel bars, for example.

The two problems you'll encounter in most aquariums (and many reptile displays in zoos) are the dim lighting and the thick glass. Though you may see people trying it, don't use on-camera flash through glass; you'll only get a picture of the reflection of your flash. With an SLR you can have a friend hold an off-camera accessory flash against the glass, but using a faster film is easier and keeps the light more natural-looking. Press the lens right up to the glass to avoid reflections.

As in the wild, animals in captivity have both active and quiet periods. Generally they are most animated early and late in the day and before feeding times. Finally, remember that captive animals of all types are already under stress; take great care not to add to it. Better to lose a shot than become another insensitive tourist.

Focal Points

- **Bring animals close with moderate telephoto lenses**
- **Disguise or exploit signs of captivity**
- **Avoid flash with glass enclosures**

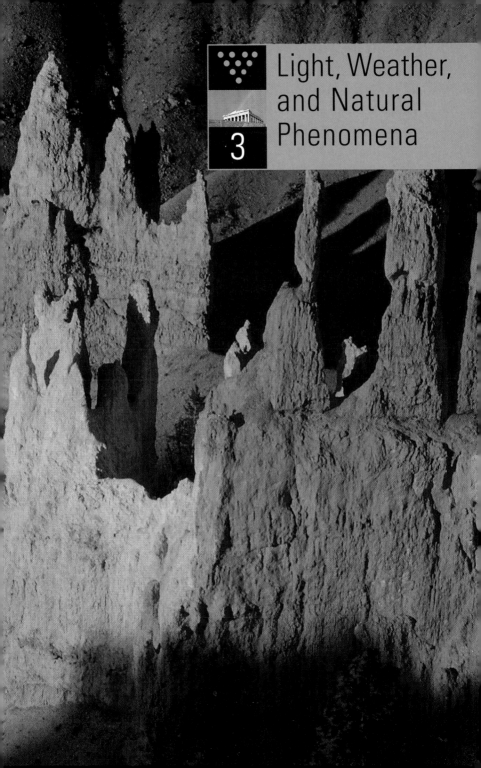

Daylight

Though we often take our cameras out into the world with the idea of recording a tree or a face or a church or a mountain range, in truth, all that we ever record is patterns of light on film. Your travel photographs are mere records of the reflection of

light. A mountain does not physically imprint its image on film, any more than the soul of a person is sucked through the lens. It is light reflecting from the mountain and the person that draws their pictures; without light, they would both still exist, but we could neither see nor record them.

More than merely illuminating the physical world, though, daylight by its changes continually reveals our surroundings anew, sometimes with utmost subtlety, sometimes with brash boldness. Rather than one static image, we are served a perpetually shifting banquet of

shapes, colors, textures, and forms, all prepared and presented by daylight. A tree that is merely a dark shape in the purple light of the predawn is revealed in infinite detail after the sun breaks the horizon and is later set aglow in the shimmering light of late afternoon: One tree, many reflections.

As a photographer, you can develop no skill more important than your ability to see and appreciate light. The three most important changes that light undergoes are in color, in direction, and in quality.

Color

From the instant when the sun begins to tinge the eastern horizon with hues of pink and gold until it sets in a blazing crimson farewell in the west, daylight constantly shifts in color. While we may notice the particularly golden light of dawn or the inky blue light of twilight, our eyes and brain tend to neutralize most gradual changes in color, so that daylight appears colorless. Color films, however, are entirely sensitive to these differences and record them faithfully. It's important, then, to learn to discern alterations in the color of daylight so you will see light the way film sees it.

The color of daylight has a profound effect on the atmosphere of a photograph, and knowing how it affects the emotional content of an image enables you to control the mood of your travel photos. A castle bathed in the cool blues and grays of twilight may seem mysterious or gloomy, perhaps even foreboding. The same castle splashed in the yellow and amber waves of early morning light appears to be safe or beckoning, summoning the reassuring memories of a favorite childhood fairy tale. Changes in daylight's color occur most rapidly— and are most dramatic—at the beginning and end of the day, so work quickly at these times if you want to capture a particular mood.

Direction of Light

The direction from which light strikes a scene, relative to the camera position, has a significant effect on color, form, texture, and depth in the resulting photo. Frontlighting spills over your shoulder and falls squarely on the front of your subject. Because frontlighting is very even, auto-exposure systems handle it well. It produces bold, saturated colors, but when too strong can actually wash out some colors. The downside is that, because all the shadows are falling behind the subject and away from the camera, frontlit scenes lack a sense of depth or three-dimensionality.

Sidelighting comes from the left or right of a subject. Because the light is scraping across from side to side, it catches every surface blip and imperfection, leaving a trail of large and small shadows and exaggerating surface textures. It is ideal for landscapes, like desert badlands or beaches, where you want to convey the tactile qualities of a subject. Sidelight also imparts form and three-dimensionality to objects, giving a pumpkin its full roundness or a tree trunk its volume. Gentle sidelighting, especially from slightly above, works well for portraits

because it creates a delicate modeling of facial features.

Backlighting can produce theatrical effects, particularly with landscapes. Shadows coming toward the camera exaggerate depth and distance and help lead the eye into the scene. When backlighting is used behind partially translucent subjects, like leaves or human hair, it creates a bright fringe called rim lighting that helps separate subjects from their surroundings. In backlit portraits, however, you may need to increase exposure by 1 to 1½ stops over the metered value to keep faces from being lost in shadow. An alternate solution is to use flash fill (see page 154). Keep the sun itself out of the frame or it will trick the meter into severe underexposure.

With many subjects, you can change

the apparent direction of lighting by changing your shooting position—by taking a short walk if you're shooting a close-up of a barn or a horse, or a drive if you're shooting a landscape.

Light Quality

Is it the hard light of a blistering sun streaming down from a clear, cloudless sky? Or the soft, diffuse light of a hazy sky soothing your subject in a soft embrace? Hard light blasts its way across the landscape, zapping subjects with brilliant highlights and creating jet-black shadow areas. Soft light awakens worlds of subtle hue and gradation and provides a gentle but pleasant modeling in both landscapes and portraits. Because you can't alter the quality of light (other than by waiting for it to change), the key is to match it to a compatible subject: hard light to accent the graphic lines of an industrial landscape, or soft light for a group portrait.

Focal Points

- **Use the changing color of daylight to establish mood**
- **Use light direction to enhance subjects' properties**
- **Match light quality to specific subjects**

Dramatic Lighting

One of the great thrills of travel photography is coming unexpectedly upon a sudden and dramatic light phenomenon—when the light's direction or color or intensity stops you in your tracks.

One autumn day I was driving in western Massachusetts looking for good foliage shots when a storm came up and the sky turned black. Just as I was waiting for lightning to start popping, a brilliant yellow shaft of sunlight shot out from the clouds and ignited the hills. It lasted just moments—I had time to shoot exactly two frames before the sun slipped away again.

As a traveler, you don't often have the luxury of waiting by a scene for a spectacular bit of lighting, but if you know when such light is likely to occur, you can be on the lookout for it. Among the best times to expect dramatic lighting are just before or after a storm. Often storms end with dozens of brilliant rays of sun bursting through a bank of clouds. Similar displays contrived by architects occur on almost any sunny day inside many cathedrals, when the sun pierces the highest windows and a thousand rays gleam down on the altar.

Another way to increase your odds is to rise before the sun and linger until long after it has set. In addition to the theatrics of sunset and sunrise (see page 94), the low-angle light of these times often brings high drama. Once, after shooting a red-rock formation in Sedona, Arizona, I was slowly packing up my gear because the sun had slipped behind a hill when its rays found a crack and suddenly washed the formations before me in a spectacular orange glow.

Such bits of dramatic illumination don't come without problems. They can be very contrasty, and the range of highlights and shadows may be beyond the capacity of your film to record. Don't try to compensate: Either use your spot-metering mode or move close physically and take an exposure reading from just the highlights.

92

Focal Points

- **Anticipate dramatic lighting events**
- **Explore before and after storms**
- **Expose for highlights and sacrifice shadow areas**

Sunrise, Sunset, and Afterglow

Sunrises and sunsets attract photographers for the simple reason that they produce lots of color and glory for very little technical effort. They also elicit a whole spectrum of emotional responses, from awe to tranquillity to romance. Though they are sometimes viewed as a trite travel subject, don't look such radiant gift horses in the mouth.

When we see a dramatic sky, we tend to point the camera up, excluding the ground entirely, but this is to overlook the potential of the event. Including a simple foreground element not only adds a center of interest but can reveal something of your location and help evoke a particular emotion or mood. A sunset over the water on Cape Cod is pretty, but place a lighthouse in the foreground and you tell a story of a particular place captured at a dramatic instant. For romance, add a hand-holding couple strolling the beach. Remember, though, that most foreground subjects are cast into silhouette when photographed against a bright sky, so look for clean and quickly recognizable shapes.

For sunsets and sunrises, a variety of different exposures will provide acceptable results. Be especially careful to keep the sun out of the frame while you take a meter reading: Aim the lens at a bright area of sky just to the left or right of the sun itself; either set this reading manually, or use your exposure lock to hold the setting and then recompose to include the sun if you want it. With slide films, I bracket by at least a full stop over and under this setting for a choice of color saturations.

Don't put your camera away immediately after the sun disappears. On partly cloudy days, especially, the sky may be suddenly and briefly illuminated with color several minutes after the sun has set—the afterglow phenomenon. Expose for afterglow by taking a reading from any area of colorful sky.

Focal Points

- **Include a simple foreground**
- **Exclude the sun when setting your exposure**
- **After sunset, wait for the afterglow to color the sky**

Rainbows

If there's a silver lining for travelers enduring a rainy morning or afternoon, it's the potential for spotting one of nature's most charming phenomena, a rainbow. Elusive, ethereal, and always cheerful, rainbows can spark a feeling of mystery and romance in even the most jaded of souls.

You may not be able to predict where a rainbow will occur, but you can increase your chance of seeing one by facing away from the sun toward the dark opposing sky after a storm. The best time to plan your rainbow shot is not after but during the storm. Use the rain time to scout around for potential compositions. Pictures of rainbows dangling in an open sky are pretty, but including an interesting foreground, such as the temple shown above, imparts a sense of scale and place.

Exposure is straightforward. If you're using color negative film, the exposure that the camera sets will be fine; if the rainbow is too light in the final print, ask your lab to redo the shot and darken it up. With slide film, use your camera's exposure-compensation feature to underexpose by a half or a full stop for more saturated color bands. If your camera has a manual exposure

96

system, take a light reading from the sky near the rainbow and then underexpose by a half or a full stop.

Here's a trick even some pros don't know about: Because rainbows are made of myriad tiny droplets of water that are reflecting light, you can use a polarizing filter (see page 176) to modulate the intensity of the colors. Simply mount the filter to the front of your SLR lens and, as you rotate it, watch in the viewfinder as the color bands brighten and then fade. Shoot when you see the saturation you want. Beware, though: In the wrong position, the filter will completely erase the colors. Also, polarizers reduce light by about 1⅓ stops, so you may want to switch to a faster film or mount your camera on a tripod.

Focal Points

- **Find rainbows by facing away from the sun after a storm**
- **Use your auto-exposure mode**
- **With an SLR, use a polarizing filter to deepen colors**

Fog and Mist

Of all weather phenomena, fog and mist are among the most powerful in evoking emotion. The reactions they elicit often vary from person to person: The soft morning mist rising above the Irish countryside that stirs feelings of serenity in you may bring on a twinge of melancholy in your companion.

Like brazen, daylight thieves, both fog and mist steal away colors, textures, and shapes, reducing · scenes to a muted palette of hues and simple, detailless forms. It's important, then, to build your compositions around subjects that can hold their own. Rather than try to capture a broad landscape, seek out the stark shapes of a lone tree and a stone wall. The farther subjects are from your camera, the more they will lose their impact, so be sure to place the most important subjects closest to the camera—a barn in the foreground of a farm scene, for example.

The reflective brightness of fog and mist fool most autoexposure systems into allowing for more light than is actually available, so you'll have to *increase* exposure over your camera's recommendation. If your camera has an exposure compensation dial, use it to add an extra stop (+1). With manual-exposure cameras and some point-and-shoots, you can create the same compensation by setting an ISO speed that's half the actual speed of the film you're using. This will provide an extra stop of exposure; remember to set it back to the correct speed once the fog or mist has burned off.

Long telephoto lenses compress the effects of fog and mist; the longer the lens, the more pronounced the compression will be. When shooting mountain landscapes, photographers often use lenses 300 mm or longer to accentuate an effect called atmospheric perspective (see page 50), which amplifies the sense of distance in mountain shots.

Focal Points

- **Use bold shapes as focal points**
- **Add extra exposure manually or use exposure compensation**
- **Choose long lenses to heighten fog and mist effects**

In the Rain

A prediction of rain doesn't have to mean the end to photography. In fact, rain produces unexpected and pleasing picture possibilities. Because it paints smooth surfaces like leaves and pavement with a glossy sheen, it lends landscapes and city street scenes a bright, pearly glow and creates deep, saturated colors. Use a polarizing filter to further saturate colors by removing surface reflections. In the city, especially at twilight or night, puddles and wet pavement transform mundane street scenes into colorful, impressionistic tableaux with reflections of neon signs and other city lights. Bracket your exposures one stop over and under the camera's recommendation.

In heavy downpours the rain itself can become the subject: At shutter speeds of 1/125th or faster you can halt the rain droplets; at slow speeds (1/30th or slower) you can turn them into long diagonal streaks cutting through the frame. Focus falling rain against a dark background to make it stand out.

Whatever the subject, it's important to protect your camera gear. If you

don't have someone to hold an umbrella over you, you can carry a few locking plastic bags to use as temporary waterproof housings. With an SLR, just put the camera into the bag, cut a hole for the lens to poke through, and secure the bag to the front rim of the lens barrel with an elastic band. You can jury-rig a similar protection for point-and-shoot cameras; just be sure that the bag doesn't block any exposure or autofocus windows on the front of the camera. In his book *Landscape Photography*, noted nature photographer John Shaw offers this unusual tip: Use a shower cap to protect a tripod-mounted camera and lens while you scout locations and then remove it briefly to shoot.

If you're traveling to a place where you're likely to encounter significant rainfall, you might also buy a plastic-bag-type underwater housing (see page 70) for your camera. Alternatively, you can take along a few one-time-use waterproof cameras.

Focal Points

- **Explore puddles and wet pavement for abstract designs**
- **Control rain-streaking with shutter speed**
- **Protect cameras with plastic bags or waterproof housings**

Lightning

Lightning, like rainbows, produces a dramatic but unpredictable show in the sky. Unlike the sweet prettiness of a rainbow, the connotations of lightning are of danger, power, and gloom. As those who are careless about being outdoors in an electrical storm sometimes find out, lightning can deliver on its threat of danger. You should photograph lightning only from a distance and preferably from inside a building or a car. If you're outdoors, seek shelter the minute a storm begins to approach. You'll probably also need to concern yourself with keeping your camera and yourself dry (see page 100) if you're outside.

You can photograph lightning day or night, though night shots are generally more productive. In daylight, the technique is simple: With your camera on a tripod and aimed at a likely sector of sky, wait for a large bolt and fire. Base your exposure on the existing light conditions, using a small aperture and the longest shutter speed available. The odds are slim that you'll catch a spectacular streak, but it's possible.

Your chances of creating a thrilling lightning shot increase dramatically after dark. You can make exposures ranging from several seconds to several minutes and record a series of bolts. An upper-floor hotel window with a city view is a good and safe vantage point. The method is simple but requires that your camera have a B setting and that you use a locking cable release and a lens cap or a small sheet of black cardboard. Here's how it works: With your camera on a tripod, compose around a simple foreground with a large area of open sky. Set the camera's shutter speed dial to the B position and lock the shutter open using your cable release. Keep a lens cap or the black cardboard over the lens until you see a flash, uncover the lens and then recover it, and wait for the next flash. Once you have several bolts on the same frame, close the shutter, advance to the next frame, and try it again. Exposure isn't critical; use an aperture of around *f*/5.6 (with an ISO 100 film) to start, and then bracket by changing the aperture.

Focal Points

- **Photograph from a safe location**
- **In daylight, expose for existing light**
- **At night, leave the shutter open during several flashes**

Putting It All Together

4

Simplify

Trying to pack too much information into a photograph is like cramming too much into your suitcase: It only makes the thing you're looking for that much harder to find. A good photograph—travel or otherwise—should reveal a single subject or idea with as little clutter as possible. It's okay if someone looking at your travel photos asks where they were taken, but if he or she has to ask what they are pictures of, you're on shaky ground, photographically speaking.

Paring your compositions down to their bare bones begins as a mental process. Try to describe in a single sentence what it is you're photographing: "This is a photograph of a lighthouse at sunset." Then begin to eliminate all but the essential visual elements. Do you need the kids on the sandbar in the foreground to make the picture? Or the boat dock in the background?

One way to isolate subjects is to experiment with different angles of view. Often shooting from an elevated vantage point will help you eliminate distracting or cluttered backgrounds, while getting down on your belly and shooting from ground level will let you isolate subjects against the sky. Another way to

subdue a busy background is to use a technique called selective focus (see page 168), which puts everything except your main subject out of focus. Of course, if your subject is movable (like a person), you can always move it to simpler surroundings.

Yet another technique for clarifying your message is to silhouette (see page 126) a subject by photographing it against a brightly lit background— a fisherman at sunset—so its shape is instantly identifiable. In the following pages we'll delve deeper into these and other ways to help unload your excess visual baggage.

Focal Points

- **Limit compositions**
- **Isolate elements**
- **Silhouette bold shapes**

Get Closer

There's an old adage in photography that says if you want to improve your photographs 100 percent, move closer. It's true. The one sure way to keep from including too much extraneous information in a photograph is to fill the frame with your subject and nothing but your subject. Filling the frame from edge to edge leaves little doubt about what your intended target was. There are two ways to get closer: Use a telephoto lens (see page 172) or put some more wear on your walking shoes.

The simple act of making your subject bigger in the frame involves the viewer at a much more intense level. A chin-to-forehead portrait of an interesting face, for example, immediately puts the viewer eye-to-eye with your subject. A very tight shot of a bear—even if you made it with a long lens at the zoo—creates breathless drama.

A common problem here is that we often *think* we're filling the frame when in fact we're not even close. If the guy at your local one-hour lab had a nickel for every time he's heard a customer say, "Gee, that waterfall seemed so close in person but it looks so far away in my pictures," he'd be the one doing all the exotic

traveling. What's happening is that when you're standing in front of a scene, you're concentrating so intently on your subject that your brain is tricked into thinking your subject is closer than it actually is.

The solution? As soon as you think you're close enough to your subject, take a few steps forward (provided you're not on the rim of the Grand Canyon) and try again. Just before you snap the shutter, roll your eye around the frame and see if there's anything you can eliminate. When in doubt, take a few more steps closer.

Focal Points
- **Fill the frame tightly for maximum impact**
- **Move closer physically or use a long lens**
- **Continually check the viewfinder for wasted space**

Choosing a Format

Among the most basic decisions that face you in composing any photograph is whether to frame it horizontally or vertically. Because cameras are rectangular and are more comfortable to hold horizontally, that's exactly how most people compose their pictures. Turning the camera on end makes handling a bit awkward, but the effort will add power and desperately needed visual variety to your pictures. Imagine how boring it would be to go to an art gallery and see only horizontal paintings.

Many subjects cry out to be framed in a particular way. As a rule, tall subjects (like trees or people), or those in which you want to exaggerate near-to-far distance, stand more comfortably in a vertical frame. Framing a scene vertically forces the eye to scan the photograph from bottom to top (and vice versa), which exaggerates the impression of depth and distance. Wide scenes or long, squat subjects lie naturally in a horizontal composition. Horizontal compositions draw the eye from side to side across the frame, reinforcing the sense of width and spaciousness.

For many subjects, either format will work; choosing the best framing is then largely a matter of instinct. In composing the two views shown here of the medieval walled city of Dinkelsbühl, Germany, I chose the vertical framing for the shot of the single tower because I wanted to accent its height and isolate it from its surroundings. In the more distant shot, I chose horizontal framing because I wanted to show a broader view and it simply looked more natural. If deciding which format looks best becomes difficult, photograph it both ways and decide later; it's often easier to grasp the full impact from a print than it is when you're looking through the viewfinder.

Though we may not always be aware of it, format also deeply affects the psychological content of a scene. Subjects framed vertically, for instance, often seem more aggressive and less stable: Skyscrapers loom overhead and trees totter in the wind. Conversely, horizontally framed subjects offer a sense of equilibrium and stability.

Focal Points

- Add variety by mixing horizontal and vertical shots
- Choose the format that gives the subject greatest drama
- Consider the psychological apects of altering format

Placing the Horizon

In outdoor photography, where in the frame you place the horizon line has a powerful effect on how your compositions are interpreted. Shifting horizon placement by tilting the camera up or down can alter the entire balance of a scene.

Placing the horizon high in the frame, for example, accents foreground details and enhances the sense of distance. Take care when using expansive foregrounds to get as much depth of field (see page 168) as possible. If your SLR camera has an aperture-priority mode, use it to set a small aperture (*f*/11 or smaller) to ensure maximum near-to-far sharpness. Some SLR and point-and-shoot cameras provide a landscape-exposure mode that automatically sets a small aperture for you. Shooting from a high vantage point and tilting the camera down so it is more parallel to the plane of the foreground also helps extend the range of sharp focus.

Horizons placed very low in the frame heighten the isolation of subjects at the horizon. In isolating a lone person at the bottom edge of the frame at right, the photographer has created an atmosphere of emptiness by contrasting it with the vastness of the sky. Low horizons are effective, too, for capturing dramatic skies: colorful sunset-illuminated clouds, for instance.

Dividing a composition exactly in half by placing the horizon across the middle of the frame is often considered breaking a sacrosanct design rule, but it isn't quite as serious as cheating on your income taxes. Try it. If it works—as it sometimes does in catching mirror reflections in pond or lake scenes—use it without shame.

Often not including a horizon at all is what works best. Instead of struggling to find the best placement, zoom in on a main subject and eliminate the horizon. Finally, no matter where you place the horizon, keep it level unless you're intentionally trying to rock your viewers' visual boats.

Focal Points

- **Use low horizon placement to accent sky or clouds**

- **Use high placement to emphasize distance and accent foreground elements**

- **Try eliminating the horizon**

The Rule of Thirds

Taking the time to find a pleasing and effective placement for your main subject is crucial to the success of your travel photographs. One method that artists have been using for centuries is the rule of thirds. It involves mentally dividing the viewfinder frame into thirds, both horizontally and vertically. The four lines and four intersections of these lines can then be used as invisible guidelines to help you find the most dynamic subject placements.

By locating a subject at one of the four intersections—as opposed to nailing it squarely in the center of the frame, for example—you give it added emphasis. The technique works well with all subjects but is particularly effective when you are photographing a relatively small subject surrounded by a large expanse of space or against a plain background. The visual weight of your subject balances the vast emptiness. A sailboat on a calm sea centered in the frame appears stagnant and overwhelmed by its surroundings, but if it is placed at a thirds intersection, its position fulfills our need for a dynamic visual tension.

You can also use thirds to help organize and support secondary subjects by setting them at diagonally opposite intersections— for example, placing a lone oak tree (the main subject) at the lower left juncture and the rising full moon (a secondary subject) diagonally opposite and above at the upper right intersection. Again, balance and dynamics.

Thirds divisions can also help you decide where to place the horizon. If you place it along one of the two frame divisions, you have a quick and effective shortcut for deciding how to arrange the composition. Imagine, for instance, that you're photographing a Caribbean beach scene that includes sand, sea, and sky. Placing the horizon at the upper line gives the sky one third of the frame and the foreground two thirds, accenting the beach and water. Conversely, placing it along the bottom division line accents the sky by giving it two thirds of the frame. You can use the same principle whether you're shooting horizontally or vertically.

Focal Points

- **Mentally divide the frame into vertical and horizontal thirds**
- **Place important subjects at thirds intersections**
- **Use thirds divisions to place the horizon**

Lines

You may not think of lines as being as exciting a travel subject as, say, a jungle snake slithering through the grass. But photograph that snake and you will surely have captured a distinctive—and emotionally charged—line. Nor would the idea of photographing a line in the sand seem irresistibly intriguing, unless of course, it was the sinuous line of a sand dune shifting in a desert wind.

Lines have many uses in a photograph. They can divide, unify, or accent certain parts of a composition. If they are interesting enough, they can become a visual topic in themselves: Who could resist the lines of a spider's web glistening with dew? Stay alert to catch transient lines, like shadows or shafts of light, before they disappear.

Lines lead the eye into a scene. Stand on a train platform and you'll see it's all but impossible to keep your eye from following the line of the tracks to the horizon. Parallel lines that appear to converge this way create what's known as one-

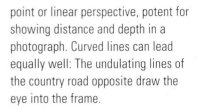

point or linear perspective, potent for showing distance and depth in a photograph. Curved lines can lead equally well: The undulating lines of the country road opposite draw the eye into the frame.

Leading lines are most effective when there is some relation between line and subject, such as winding stone steps leading to a castle door. You can exaggerate their impact further by using a wide-angle lens and finding a vantage point close to the beginning of the lines—kneeling to get close to train tracks, for example.

The shape and the direction of lines in a photograph are also forceful setters of mood. Straight lines, whether vertical or horizontal, seem stable and formal. The sharp lines of a picket fence have little sensuousness, but consider the alluring slopes of rolling hills or a tanned body lying on the beach.

Focal Points

- **Take time to notice lines**
- **Let lines lead the eye to a main subject**
- **Use the shape of lines to establish mood**

Taking Pictures Through Frames

A quick way to focus attention on a particular subject and to enhance the sensation of depth in a scene is to use some object or shape in the foreground as a frame within a frame, such as the overhanging bough that frames a landscape. Many other creative possibilities include doorways, windows, archways—almost anything that lets you look through one thing at another.

Foreground frames usually work best when they have a contextual relationship with the subject. While touring the Breakers, the famous mansion in Newport, Rhode Island, I was struck by the fantastic view of the great lawn and the ocean from the rear of the house. Straight shots of the view seemed dreadfully dull; there was no feeling of scale and no relationship to the mansion. Near the end of the tour, however, we paused on a grand balcony with soaring stone arches framing the sea view, and I knew I had found my picture.

In using frames, lens choice is important. In the case of the Breakers shot, my choice was easy: The balcony was so broad and my mobility so limited that I was forced to use a very wide 24 mm lens. It made the ocean seem more distant, but that enhanced the panoramic effect. At other times you may want to put on a medium telephoto lens and back away from the frame so you use the lens's power to compress the background and frame together—a garden statue seen through a rose-covered trellis, for example.

To keep both frame and subject in sharp focus, set a small aperture so there is sufficient depth of field. If you want only the subject sharp, use a wide aperture. Be sure that the focusing sensors (see page 161) are on the main subject and not on the frame; otherwise you'll focus on the foreground instead of the main subject. Frames work best if they are darker than your main subject, so take your light reading from the subject and let the frame fall into darkness.

Focal Points

- **Use foreground frames to draw attention to a subject**
- **Look for frames that complement the subject**
- **Expose for the subject, and let the frame go dark**

Patterns

Patterns, both natural and man-made, bring a sense of visual rhythm and harmony to photographs that, like a series of repeating notes in a melody, captures the imagination. Patterns appear whenever strong graphic elements—lines, colors, shapes, or forms—repeat themselves.

I'm often amazed at how many more pictures of patterns I take while traveling than I do at home; perhaps when we're in new and unusual surroundings, our visual sense is more alert. Once you do become aware of their power, you will discover patterns almost everywhere: in a field of Maine lupines, in crowds of faces in a stadium, even in the zigs and zags of modern architecture.

The secret to finding patterns is to explore potential subjects from a variety of angles. While you might not notice the colorful design of umbrellas as you maneuver a crowded Paris sidewalk, they become blatantly clear from an upper-floor window or balcony. Lighting is another potent painter of pattern: Fresh-plowed furrows in a cornfield, all but invisible on a dull, overcast day, rise into waves of highlight and shadow when lit by a bright, low-angle sun. Close-ups are also filled with pattern: Consider the swirl of seeds in a sunflower or the intricate tracings of color in a butterfly's wings.

The key to emphasizing patterns is to isolate them from their surroundings. By excluding everything but the design, you create the illusion that the repetition is infinite, extending beyond the frame. Telephoto and longer zoom lenses are excellent tools for isolating and extracting patterns by enabling you to exclude extraneous images.

Patterns also reinforce the emotional appeal of their components. In his book *Learning to See Creatively,* photographer Bryan Peterson observes: "Whatever emotional response a single design element arouses is multiplied when it is repeated in a pattern."

Focal Points

- **Find patterns in repeated shapes, colors, and lines**
- **Try close-ups or overviews**
- **Isolate patterns for maximum impact (use a telephoto lens)**

Textures That Touch the Eye

Look at a close-up photo of a weathered old barn board and you almost wince at the imagined pain of catching a sharp splinter. Our memories of how things feel are so ingrained in our consciousness that the mere sight of them brings a vivid sensation of touch. By exploiting textures you can bring a tactile dimension to your photographs.

Surface textures become most apparent when they are illuminated from an oblique light source. Angled light catches the shape and imperfections of an object's surface and creates a pattern of highlight and shadow to produce visual texture. The quality of the light is also important. Bold and large textures, such as the bark of a tree or the rough surface of the door detail at right, are best revealed by strong, direct sidelight. Smooth, more finely detailed textures, such as that of satin, would be erased by powerful light and are revealed best by gentler, oblique light.

Framing is important, too, especially when you want to give texture a leading role. By moving in close to an old, weathered face, either physically or with a long lens, you focus the viewer's attention on the wrinkles and crevices. When the texture is part of a broader scene, as in the surfaces of a coarse and barren desert, it's often better to back off and show its expanse. Sometimes you can dramatize texture by comparing different surfaces within a scene: an elderly potter's gnarled hands turning a vessel of wet, silken clay. In revealing such contrasts, it's important to move in close and exclude everything that doesn't enhance the tactile qualities of your image.

Black-and-white film (see page 134) is often a better choice than color in capturing texture, because it enhances the graphic qualities of your subjects and eliminates the distraction of color. In either color or black and white, use slow speed (ISO 64 or 25) to capture the tiny details that make up all textures.

Focal Points

- **Capitalize on the tactile qualities of subjects**
- **Use oblique lighting to heighten surface textures**
- **Compare a variety of textures within a shot**

Dramatic Angles

Surprise is an important ingredient in a good travel photograph, and photographing your subjects from unexpected angles is a simple way to add the unexpected. Most of us tend to spot and snap potential subjects from an eye-level, straight-ahead point of view. We look down at tulips, out at the sea, and up at skyscrapers. By exploring your subjects beyond predictable first impressions, you can create new and startling compositions.

This requires a bit of visual detective work: You have to walk (or crawl or climb) around, over, and under your subject until its true personality surfaces. You may feel silly in getting to such vantage points, but your pictures will vindicate you.

High vantage points, for example, help organize complex scenes. At street level, faces and signs in a crowded marketplace dominate, making the scene chaotic. From a balcony or window above, however, crates of colorful fruits and vegetables form patterns, and streaming crowds weave inviting visual rhythms.

Low angles can exaggerate the height of tall subjects or reveal unseen aspects of low-lying ones, especially when combined with a very close viewpoint and the perspective-stretching effects of a wide-angle lens. A photograph of the Statue of Liberty from a normal viewpoint with a normal lens looks, well, normal. But move up next to the base with a 24 mm or wider lens and shoot straight up, and it becomes a soaring tower of converging angles.

A shift in lateral position or any extreme viewpoint can also produce dramatic angles. In her book *Vineyard Summer,* a portrait of life on Martha's Vineyard, photographer Alison Shaw has a thrilling shot of a ketch taken as she looked back at the bow from a precarious perch on the bowsprit. It perfectly captures the feeling of a boat surging through the sea.

Focal Points

- **Try dramatic angles to make ordinary subjects exciting**
- **Use high angles to help organize chaos and uncover patterns and low angles to exaggerate height**

Silhouettes

If you've ever slowed your car when you've seen the outline of a bounding deer on a yellow road sign, you know the immediate power shapes have in identifying objects. In photography, the simplest and most effective way to reveal a shape is by creating a silhouette. You can use silhouettes in your travel pictures to dramatize subjects whenever shape is more important than form or texture, or just to jazz up your slide shows.

To create silhouettes, simply put an opaque object in front of a bright background and expose for the background. Any brightly colored surface will work: a glittering gold sea at sunset, a cheerful colored wall, or even the illuminated glass wall of an aquarium. Rarely, however, do elegant coincidences of interesting subject and colorful background just appear. More often, you'll have to use your artist's eye to spot the potential of a bright background and then hunt around until you match it with a suitable foreground subject.

Look for subjects that have a bold and simple shape. It's important too that the subject be entirely surrounded by the bright background. A fisherman on the beach at sunrise will produce a clearly identifiable shape, but fishing boats lined up too closely in a row may merge into a dark clump.

Exposing for silhouettes is fairly simple; as with sunsets, a variety of exposures will produce good results. If your camera has an averaging meter (as do most point-and-shoots), be sure to skew the viewfinder toward the brighter area and then use your exposure-lock feature to hold that exposure. If you have an SLR that has a spot-metering feature, take a reading of just the bright area and then bracket in half- or full-stop increments toward overexposure.

Focal Points

- **Silhouette bold shapes against bright backgrounds**
- **Meter and expose for the background illumination**
- **Don't let conflicting shapes converge**

Abstract Compositions

No rule in photography says every picture you take must be a completely literal translation of your subject. Indeed, many of the most alluring travel photographs break from reality and offer an interpretive or even totally abstract vision of the world. Because travel itself is often a surreal and fragmented experience, occasional forays into abstraction may be the best way to capture the true spirit of a trip. There are no rights or wrongs: You can simply let your imagination run wild.

Where to find fodder for *your* abstract ambitions? After a rain, reflections from wet sidewalks and puddles produce myriad impressionistic images. At twilight, when neon store signs and traffic lights begin to glow, wet asphalt becomes a luminous billboard of color. Look also to the fractured, mosaic-like mirror of city life found in the glass-and-steel facades of modern buildings.

Striking abstract subjects can emerge from well-observed (though often overlooked) confluences of color, shape, texture, and form that are the components of larger scenes. Pioneer color photographer Ernst Haas, one of the masters of abstract color photography, had an intense

affection for peculiarly shaped fragments of peeling paint, torn billboard posters, and even crushed beer cans. Another master of photographic abstraction, Pete Turner, frequently finds his colorful compositions in the odd shapes and contrasting colors of such ordinary things as plastic garbage cans and beach umbrellas.

Whatever the source of the design, as with patterns, the secret to finding and capturing powerful abstracts is isolation—extracting the components of your images from their surroundings completely enough so the design and not the individual object or objects becomes your subject. Keep in mind, though, that not everyone will see the same beauty in your flights of visual whimsy that you do; don't be too offended by quizzical stares when you pass your snaps around at the office.

Focal Points

- **Don't restrict yourself to realistic renderings**
- **Look for ideas in reflections, shapes, and colors**
- **Keep designs simple**

Establishing Size

One of the primary differences between looking at a scene in person and looking at a photograph of it is that in person you have numerous cues as to the size of objects. A cow, a car, or a pumpkin somewhere in the scene helps shape your sense of scale. When you compose a photograph, though, you eliminate many of these clues, leaving viewers to wonder about the size of objects; subjects that appear only inches tall may in reality be enormous, and vice versa. The more unusual or obscure the subject is, the less able we are to judge its true size without help.

While almost any object of known size will provide such cues, the human form is perhaps the most universal indicator. In the photograph of the giant hand opposite, for example, it would be impossible to guess its true magnitude without having the children as a measuring stick.

What to do if there are no size cues handy? Creative use of framing can

indicate size. In photographing a lone pine tree, for instance, you can make it seem larger by moving closer to it and filling the frame; or, you can move farther away and make it appear more diminutive by giving it less space in the frame.

You can easily turn the tables on reality by using your knowledge of size recognition. One method is to use a wide-angle lens close to a foreground subject to make it appear to loom over a much larger object in the background—as in the girl seeming to reach out and touch the Taj Mahal above. It's important when using this technique to set as small an aperture as possible to keep both foreground and background in sharp focus.

Alternatively, you can disguise the scale of a scene altogether by eliminating any visual cues to size. Abstract images often work best when the viewer is left without any hint of the real dimensions of a scene.

Focal Points

- **Include objects of known size**
- **Use people for scale, where possible**
- **Experiment with false or misleading scale**

Color

Colors, more than any other design element, determine the emotional content of a photograph. You can establish the entire mood of a shot by emphasizing a particular color scheme: Reds and oranges are hot and exciting, ready to burn at the touch. Blues and greens are cool and refreshing, the deep runnings of a mountain stream or the freshness of new-mown lawn. Yellows warm us, from the buttery glow of morning sunlight to the romantic amber of candlelight.

You can also use colors to create specific effects. With careful framing and camera angle, you can draw attention to a relatively small but brightly colored subject against a more subdued background—an Indian woman in a colorful sari walking down a dusty path, for example. The danger inherent in color is that unless you are careful in composing your images, bright patches of color may divert the eye to minor parts of a scene.

Vibrant contrasts, particularly among bright primary colors (reds, yellows, and blues), are especially effective in creating dynamic designs. Such contrasts excite the eye, making it jump from one color to the next. In the shot of buoys, for example, the

photographer has eliminated all extraneous information so the clash between colors is the predominant design element. Gentler combinations of pastels can create a lighthearted or romantic mood, while earthy tones offer a more natural or organic feel.

Whatever the use of color, weather, lighting, and exposure all influence how colors photograph. Bright, sunny days are good when you want to zap your images with Day-Glo brilliance, while overcast days produce subtle, more saturated color combinations. Exposure, too, affects colors. With color slide film, especially, you can intensify colors by underexposing a full stop below the suggested meter reading. Conversely, you can subdue colors by overexposing by a half to a full stop.

Focal Points

- **Accentuate mood through color**
- **Highlight subjects or create designs through color contrasts**
- **Study the effects of weather and lighting**

Black-and-White

Though the idea of working in black-and-white may seem a tad old-fashioned, reducing the world to a palette of grays has a number of creative benefits. By wiping away the superficial veneer of color, black-and-white films unleash a world of line, shape, texture, and form that color films often disguise. Black-and-white pictures also have an inherently journalistic look, which forces viewers to give more serious consideration to the content of your images—an important point if you want to add social commentary to your travel pictures.

Black-and-white films do not record the world in the same way that color films—or our eyes—see it. While they are sensitive to all the colors of the spectrum, they are more sensitive to some (particularly blue) and less so to others (greens and reds). If you are photographing a red barn in a green field with a blue sky, the sky will be very light, while the barn and grass will record as much deeper shades of gray. Also, because the red and green sensitivites of black-and-white film are similar, the barn and grass will record as much the same tone.

If you own an SLR and a few colored filters, it's easy to manipulate the way black-and-white films record different colors. Filters enable you to reestablish a more natural-looking contrast by controlling how much light of each particular color strikes the film. The basic rule to remember is this: Filters lighten objects of their own color and darken opposites. A yellow filter, for example, will lighten the tone of a yellow dress while slightly darkening a blue hat. A red filter will cause a red barn to record as a much lighter shade of gray but will make both green grasses and blue skies record very dark.

One other advantage of shooting in black-and-white is that it's not very complicated or expensive to get started in processing and printing your own pictures at home—and create a whole new range of special effects.

Focal Points

- **Emphasize graphic elements with monochromatic tones**
- **Manipulate tonal response through colored filters**
- **Consider processing your own pictures**

Black-and-White Infrared

If you'd like to take a surreal step deeper into black-and-white photography, consider experimenting with Kodak high-speed infrared film. In addition to being sensitive to much of the visible spectrum, it has an extra layer of emulsion that records invisible infrared light. Subjects that reflect a lot of infrared record as very bright in the final image; because we can't see infrared, we have no way to predict what effect it will have in our pictures. The results are always surprising and often have an other-worldly look.

Many natural subjects, like leaves and grass, that reflect a lot of infrared take on a highly luminous and hauntingly abstract appearance with infrared film. Summer landscapes often look covered in snow. You can add even more drama to daylight scenes by placing a red filter over the lens: Blue skies will turn near black, while clouds (which have particles that reflect infrared) will become shimmering white cotton puff balls.

There are some important precautions to keep in mind when using infrared film. It must be loaded and unloaded in total darkness (a windowless hotel bathroom with all the lights turned off is dark enough)

and returned to its original container after use—not too convenient if you want to change to another film while in the field. You can, however, load and unload film in the field if you use a portable, light-proof "changing bag" designed for this.

Remember that infrared film is experimental, so bracket your exposures and be sure to have your film processed by a lab that has worked with infrared before. Also, because not all point-and-shoot cameras are infrared-proof (that is, they may be susceptible to infrared-light leaks), read your camera manual (or call the manufacturer) to be sure the camera is infrared safe. Most SLRs are safe for infrared films.

Because the light does not focus at the same plane as visible light, you must sometimes make a focusing adjustment (most SLR lenses have an infrared focusing index mark to guide you in this correction) or at least use a small aperture to ensure maximum sharpness.

Focal Points

- **Use infrared for abstract, impressionistic effects**
- **Load and unload film in total darkness**
- **Enhance the deep sky effect with red filters**

Existing
Light and
Flash

5

Existing Light Indoors

Because much of our vacation time is spent indoors—in hotel rooms, restaurants, museums—it's important to know how to shoot in these situations. Yes, it's usually possible to put on a flash and light up even the darkest of places, but the indiscriminate blast of flash destroys the intimate mood of existing light, whether it's daylight or artificial lighting. With fast films (ISO 400 to 1600), a fast lens (*f*/2.8 or faster), and a tripod, you can shoot in even the dimmest ambient illumination without flash.

Museum and other interiors lit by daylight are often bright enough that you can work at handheld shutter speeds and still get a natural color balance. Window light also has a soft, even quality that is good for casual portraits; be sure, however, to position yourself to shoot *with* rather than into the light, or it will fool your meter into underexposing your subject's face.

When shooting pictures indoors by artificial light, you will have to make a decision about color quality. Because most color films are balanced for daylight, which is very blue (see page 86), and incandescent (tungsten) lighting is more red, pictures taken by artificial lighting on

daylight film will have a warm overall tone. With color negative film, some of the warmth can be taken out during printing, but it does give pictures a more intimate and realistic look. If color balance is critical, switch to a tungsten-balanced color slide film.

Often when shooting indoors, you'll work with a mixture of natural and artificial lighting, and the results can be evocative. In taking an informal portrait by a window in a pub, for instance, you might have daylight from a window, a lamp on a nearby wall, and a candle at the table. The color balance will be natural in the areas lit by daylight but have a warm glow in areas lit by the lamp and candles. The absolute worst artificial lighting to shoot by is fluorescent, because pictures usually come out a sickly shade of green. Avoid it when possible. If you must shoot with it, you can use a light pink FLD filter with daylight films to remove some of the greenish cast.

140

Focal Points

- **Avoid flash; use fast film and a fast lens**
- **Take advantage of soft window lighting**
- **Try using daylight-balanced color-negative film**

Museums

Museums can range from obscure little rooms with a specific theme (like the terrific swordfishing museum on Martha's Vineyard that's nothing more than a wooden shanty) to grand architectural statements housing the world's great artworks. Most will allow some photography (call ahead and ask), but there are usually restrictions about using tripods and flash, so you must frequently rely on fast films. Even when flash is allowed, I would use it only in desperation. Most museums invest considerable time and money in lighting design, so why mock it with flash?

Whether you use daylight or tungsten-balanced film will depend largely on the architecture of the museum and how accurate you need the colors to be in your prints. Some museums have large areas lit by windows or skylights (usually in sculpture rooms, where fading is less of a concern), and using daylight film will provide natural colors. If the main lighting is from tungsten fixtures, however, the colors will turn out much warmer than they appear to your eye, and this may distract from the artwork or display. Again, if color accuracy is important, switch to a tungsten-balanced slide film.

The best photo subjects in museums are usually sculptures, dioramas (in natural-history museums), and overall room views. Getting a quality shot of a painting is difficult, so it's better just to hit the postcard or poster rack and buy copies of your favorite works. If you're unfamiliar with the museum, bring several lenses: a wide-angle (around 28 mm) for overall views or when space is tight, a normal lens for close-ups, and a medium telephoto (85 mm to 105 mm) for shooting details from a distance.

The matter of picture-taking etiquette is very serious in museums. People come from great distances to spend just a few hours in a museum; it's important to respect their concentration and privacy. Work as quickly and quietly as possible, and if you notice anyone becoming annoyed, move on and return later.

Focal Points

- **Call in advance regarding photo restrictions**
- **Match film to light source when color is critical**
- **Bring several lenses or a zoom**

Stage Shows and Events

Stage shows and other theatrical events are a popular part of travel itineraries and, when photography is allowed, provide a chance to bring home professional-looking pictures. They are, however, among the most difficult photographic subjects you'll encounter. The two major obstacles are low light levels and limited stage access.

You can overcome some of the problems of low light by using a fast film in the ISO 400 to 1000 range, but even then you're likely to be working at very slow shutter speeds. Because stage performances are rarely static events, you're bound to get some motion. One solution is to watch the performance long enough to get a feel for when there will be lulls in the action and shoot at those instants. Sometimes it's better and less frustrating simply to accept a certain degree of subject blur—or even exaggerate it by using longer-than-necessary shutter speeds.

Stage lighting is also tricky to expose for, with bright spotlights hitting some parts of a stage and other areas falling into darkness. The best solution: Use a telephoto lens to isolate an individual performer, and take your meter reading from that person's face. Be especially careful

not to let bright spotlights or very dark surroundings into the frame—either will mislead the meter. Incidentally, flash is rarely allowed; even if it is, I don't recommend it, as it destroys the beauty of the theatrical lighting.

As to stage access, occasionally you'll have plenty of mobility and will be able to approach the stage or performance area freely. More commonly, if you want close-up shots, you'll have to work from a distance using a telephoto lens. In some cases, like the shot of the bagpipers with the castle at right, you may even want to switch to a wide-angle lens to include more of the overall setting.

Remember, too, that if the stage lighting is very dim, your autofocus system (see page 161) may have difficulty finding sharp focus, so you may need to switch to a manual-focus mode if that's available.

144

Focal Points

- **Never use flash**
- **Shoot with fast (ISO 400 to 1000) film**
- **Use telephoto lenses**
- **Focus manually if necessary**

Lights at Night

If you're willing to go exploring with fast films and/or a tripod, the after-dark world is rife with bright and colorful subjects. Neon lights, theatrically lighted landmarks and monuments, and carnivals all present picture opportunities that don't show up by daylight.

The stripes and squiggles of neon lights and signs are among my favorite nighttime subjects; they're colorful and provide good results over a wide range of exposures. Often, too, the lights are bright enough for making handheld exposures with a moderate-speed film, typically 1/60 second at *f*/4 with ISO 200 film. Sometimes individual signs work as a whole, but more often you'll create stronger images by moving in close to isolate patterns or abstract designs within a sign. In places like Las Vegas or Times Square, where neon propagates with wild abandon, use a telephoto lens's ability to compress space to squeeze a number of lights into a brilliant fanfare. For the Las Vegas strip photo shown here, I used a 200 mm lens and shot down from a hotel window.

Carnivals and amusement parks abound with night lights. You can get a bird's-eye view by climbing aboard a Ferris wheel, as the photographer

did for the unusual shot at center right. Lighting will be fairly dim, so use a very fast (ISO 1000 or 1600) film for sharp handheld pictures or use a tripod and long shutter speeds at ground level to capture the motion of the rides (see page 180).

Bridges, fountains, and monuments are often more interesting to photograph at night, when they are theatrically lighted and the darkness hides distracting or unattractive surroundings. Use a tripod to steady the camera, and make long exposures so you can use small apertures for maximum depth of field. Exposure isn't critical; move in close, take readings of just the lighted areas (or use your spot-metering mode), and bracket a stop or two in both directions. In any nighttime situation, color negative films will provide the greatest exposure forgiveness. Don't worry about getting a correct color balance; the potpourri of light sources creates some very pretty effects.

Focal Points

- **Move in close on neon signs**
- **Capture lights from unusual vantage points**

Fireworks

Photographing a fireworks display is similar to photographing an electrical storm (see page 102), but you have the advantage of knowing approximately when and where the bursts of light will occur.

If you're using an SLR, you have a few different exposure options. For handheld shots, load your camera with an ISO 400 film, wait for the peak of a burst, aim, and fire. An exposure of 1/60 second at *f*/2.8 is a good starting point with bright, nearby displays. If your camera has a multiple-exposure button, you can use it to gather several bursts onto a single frame.

For a more striking effect, borrow the technique used for capturing bolts of lightning: With the camera on a tripod, open the shutter on B, set the aperture to *f*/8, and capture a series of bursts on one frame. This technique lets you trace the path of the bursts as their colors sear the night sky; the disadvantage is that you have to guess where the bursts will occur before you open the shutter. With either method, using a wide-angle lens will provide room for framing error.

Because most point-and-shoots lack both a B setting and multiple-exposure capability, the best option

is simply to load up with medium- or high-speed film, set the autofocus to infinity, and shoot single exposures at the peak of each burst.

You can almost always improve a fireworks shot by including something in the foreground: either a partial silhouette, like a city skyline or heads in a crowd, or a lighted monument, like the Statue of Liberty. Two other tips: A small flashlight will help you see camera controls better, and don't forget to save several frames for the finale!

Focal Points

- **Shoot individual bursts using a handheld camera**

- **Capture several explosions with a time exposure**

- **Include an interesting foreground**

Around the Campfire

If you're planning a wilderness trip, fear not: The rich and ruddy glow of the campfire can be an equally evocative conveyor of atmosphere. The cozy mood of people relaxing around the flames is ideal for informal portraits. A tripod is a good idea for very sharp pictures, but you can take handheld shots using fast film if you steady the camera on a rock or a fencepost.

Whether or not you want the fire itself in your shots, be careful not to include it when you take your meter reading, because the flames will fool the camera into grossly under-exposing your subjects. Instead, use your spot-metering mode to take readings directly from a well-lighted face; alternatively, move in close and fill the frame with just a face. This will provide good exposure setting for skin tones, though it may tend to wash out the colors of the fire. You can take a second reading of just the flames; setting an exposure that's midway between the two readings will keep faces well exposed while retaining the intensity of the flames.

With many autofocus cameras, the exposure and focus locks may be linked. If you move in to get physically closer to take a face reading and lock that reading, then the focus also locks at that distance. When you back up to recompose a wider picture, your subject will be out of focus. Using a zoom lens can get around this by zooming in on a subject's face, locking the exposure and focus, then zooming wider to take your picture. Changing the zoom setting does not affect the focus position with most cameras.

In any event, be sure your subject's face is evenly lighted by the fire, or ask her or him to turn toward the flames so that it is. If there are lanterns in the scene, arrange them to provide additional fill-in lighting.

While flames are bright, the light reaching the faces isn't, so you'll need to use fairly fast (ISO 400 or 1000) film or mount your camera on a tripod. If you have a tripod and can get your subjects to sit still for an exposure of several seconds, sparks and flames streaming up from the fire will create interesting light trails.

Focal Points

- **Keep flames out of the frame when reading the meter**

- **For portraits, take spot readings of faces**

- **Use a tripod, or rest your camera on something solid**

Using Flash

Fast films and fast lenses make it easy to work in all but the most dimly lighted situations, but there are times when turning to electronic flash is a better alternative. For example, because the duration of flash is so brief (often measured in thousandths of a second), you can use it to get sharp pictures of moving subjects in very dark surroundings—like dancers in the ballroom of a cruise ship. The drawback of flash is that it produces a comparatively harsh and obtrusive light.

Most point-and-shoot and many SLR cameras have a built-in flash that is capable of producing good results over a modest distance range— typically from about three to 15 feet with an ISO 100 film. Accessory flash units for SLRs are considerably more powerful and sophisticated than built-ins, frequently providing a maximum shooting range of 100 feet or more.

Accessory flash units are mounted atop the camera and come in two types. **Automatic** flash units can be used with any camera and have front-mounted sensors that set exposures by measuring the flash

bouncing back from the subject.

Dedicated units are designed for specific brands and models of camera and use sophisticated electronic camera-to-flash communication to make all the settings for you. The camera measures the reflected flash at the film plane and shuts off the unit when correct exposure is achieved.

A problem peculiar to taking portraits with any type of electronic flash is the phenomenon known affectionately as red eye, the somewhat satanic red glint in subjects' pupils often seen in photos. The effect occurs as the flash reflects off the rear surface of the retina. Many flash units, both built-in and accessory, have a red-eye-reduction feature that uses a series of brief preflashes to constrict the pupil, thereby eliminating the effect—a feature worth paying extra for if you photograph people often.

Focal Points

- **Stop motion in low light with flash**
- **Stay within the recommended distance range**
- **Buy a flash with the red-eye reduction mode**

Fill-In Flash

Though making dark places brighter is the primary use of flash, the next-best place to use it, surprisingly enough, is outdoors in bright sunlight. One of the problems of taking pictures—especially individual or group portraits—by midday sun is that the harsh lighting creates deep, distracting shadows. In people pictures this usually means dark eye sockets and unattractive shadows under the nose and lips. Fill-in flash lightens these shadows to create more attractive portraits.

Fill-in flash looks most natural when it's about a stop darker than the main light. When the flash-to-daylight ratio is too even, or when flash overpowers the existing light, the balance looks false and draws attention to the fact that you used flash. Until the advent of built-in and dedicated accessory flash, making the calculations for fill-in flash was like doing the math for sending a rocket into another galaxy. It was easier (and quicker) to wait for a hazy day.

Today, most built-in and dedicated flash units have a special mode just for fill-in flash. Basically, all you do is point and shoot. The camera reads the ambient lighting and then kicks out just enough flash to fill shadows

but leave the picture natural-looking. Many dedicated accessory flash units even let you set a specific flash-to-daylight ratio, so you can make the fill more or less bright. Because a dedicated flash's output is mated to the autofocusing system, the camera even knows how far away your subject is.

If you're using an automatic accessory flash on an SLR, the procedure has a few more steps, but it's still painless. First, take a reading of your subject's highlights and set that exposure on your camera; then, using the calculator dial on your flash, set it to provide a flash equal to one stop less light. The instruction manual with your flash will provide more specific information.

Fill-in flash isn't limited to taking pictures of people: I frequently use just a gentle kiss of flash to open up the deep shadows in close-ups of flowers or architectural details.

Focal Points

- **Use flash to fill deep shadows in bright sunlight**
- **Set the fill-in light a stop darker than the ambient light**

Special Effects, Techniques, and Equipment

6

Choosing a Camera

With so many different models and brands to choose from, buying a new camera can be harder than picking a vacation spot—and you have to live with your decision a lot longer. Your primary concern will probably be whether you want to buy a single-lens reflex (SLR) or a point-and-shoot. Each has distinct advantages and disadvantages, though in some respects the lines are beginning to blur.

The prime advantage of owning an SLR has always been the availability of interchangeable lenses; from ultra-wide-angles to ultratelephotos, SLRs let you attach any lens your wallet can afford. This is still a formidable benefit. But with so many point-and-shoots now equipped with zoom lenses, optical flexibility is becoming less of an issue. Do you need interchangeable lenses? It depends. If you envision yourself becoming involved in serious architectural or wildlife photography, where an unusual range of lenses and ultimate optical quality is required, buy an

SLR. If all you want is an easy-to-use camera that offers a limited zoom range, then a point-and-shoot will do just fine.

The other outstanding feature of SLRs is that, because of the reflex viewing system, you see *exactly* what the lens sees (and what your picture will show). With point-and-shoot cameras, you look through a separate viewfinder. Here too, however, the boundaries are fading. Most zoom point-and-shoot cameras, for example, have a viewfinder that automatically adjusts your view as you zoom in or out. What you see is pretty close to (but not exactly) what you get.

From model to model, price differences are based largely on the number of features offered—a camera that offers a banquet-length menu of exposure and metering modes and a built-in flash costs more than a simpler camera. Are all those extra modes worth the money? Yes, if you're willing to study the manual and learn how and when to use them. No, if all you plan to do is stick the camera in the program mode and shoot.

158

Shooting Accessories

In figuring a budget for buying a camera, you should consider purchasing two accessories as well:

Camera cases. Travel is tough on photo equipment, so it's a good idea to buy some type of case for protecting it. The size and style will depend on how much equipment you own. A small waist pouch is a convenient way to carry a point-and-shoot and an extra roll or two of film. If you're going to be toting an SLR and a couple of lenses, a dozen rolls of film, a flash, and a few special-effects filters, you are probably a good candidate for a shoulder bag. (If you carry much more than that, you're a good candidate for visiting a chiropractor.) Buy a shoulder bag that is comfortable fully loaded and provides easy access to the gear inside. The main compartment should open and close using an oversize zipper or hook-and-eye fasteners and should keep the contents secure even if the bag turns upside down. Weather protection is important, too; at least one manufacturer makes bags with built-in rain hoods—an excellent feature if you're trekking to wet climates.

Camera supports. Whether or not you should bring a tripod with you on a trip depends on how dedicated a

shooter you are and what type of trip you're taking. On a week-long rail trip across Europe, a tripod can become an albatross, but if you're weekending by car, it won't take up much room in the trunk. The fact is, whenever you do bring one along, you will take sharper, more carefully considered pictures. Tripods enable you to use your camera's full range of shutter-speed and aperture combinations, which gives you immense control over depth of field (see page 168) and provides ultimate stability with long telephoto lenses.

Pick a tripod sturdy enough to give good support but light enough so you won't dread carrying it. It should be tall enough to let you work at eye level and steady holding the longest lens you own.

159

Camera Handling

In my office there is a 16- x 24-inch enlargement of a photograph of wild burros that I took in the desert outside Las Vegas. I used a $15 panoramic camera and a relatively fast (ISO 400) film, but the enlargement is sharp. The point is that optical and film quality are so good today that even the cheapest cameras can make acceptably sharp pictures. Why, then, are "blurry" pictures the chief complaint among casual photographers?

The answer is simple: You must hold the camera steady. More pictures have been ruined by shaky hands than all the poor lenses in the world. Whether you're using a point-and-shoot or an SLR, the best technique is to rest the camera in the palm of one hand and squeeze the shutter button gently with your free hand. Gently.

The effects of camera shake increase with telephoto lenses (or zooms set at telephoto settings), as these lenses are heavier and magnify not just your subject's size but any camera shake. Most automatic cameras are programmed to pick a sufficiently fast shutter speed and have a warning beep (and/or a light in the viewfinder) that lets you know when your speed's too slow. If you

get a warning, either switch to a higher shutter speed or, if that's not an option, find something to rest the camera on—a fence post or porch rail, for example. Another solution is to use a tripod or monopod (see page 159), which is something you might consider, especially if you're traveling by car and have a place to stow it.

Autofocus Techniques

Another ingredient of sharp images is focusing the camera carefully. Back in the ancient days of photography, a decade or so ago, focusing a camera meant laboriously twisting the lens barrel until the image in the viewfinder was in sharp focus. Autofocus (AF) technology today has made focusing as painless as pressing a button; still, to increase your percentage of sharp pictures, keep a few things in mind before you press it.

All autofocus systems, for example, require that you place your subject at the center of the viewfinder, because that's where the focusing sensors are. What if you decide to get a little artistic by putting your subject, say, a tad off-center? No problem; AF systems have a focus-lock feature (usually activated by partially depressing the shutter button) that lets you focus with your subject in the center, lock focus, then recompose to put it where you want it.

Most AF cameras offer two focusing modes: single-shot and continuous. If your subject is one that sits still (like a landscape or a very good dog), the single-shot mode is better, because it will not fire the shutter until it finds sharp focus. If you're trying to snag a

moving target (like a racehorse or a not-so-patient dog), switch to the continuous mode, and the camera will continuously refocus until the instant of exposure. In this mode, however, the shutter will fire whether or not your subject is sharp.

Most point-and-shoot cameras use an "active" AF system that bounces an infrared light beam off subjects, while most SLR cameras use a "passive" system that focuses by measuring subject contrast to determine subject distance. The advantage of active systems is that you can use them in virtual darkness as they provide their own focusing light; their disadvantage is that they are not as precise.

Passive systems are more accurate but require a certain level of contrast to focus and may have trouble focusing on subjects of low contrast, such as a white wall or a foggy harbor, forcing you to resort to a manual-focus mode.

161

Focal Points

- **Focus with your main subject centered**
- **Use your focus-lock feature to move subjects off center**
- **Switch to manual focus in low light and low contrast**

Exposure Basics

Exposure is the amount of light that it takes to record a scene correctly on film. Give the film too much light and the picture will look washed out, too little light and it will be lost in murky darkness. Virtually all point-and-shoot and most SLR cameras employ tiny computer chips to set the exposure automatically, often without so much as a prayer from you. Still, having some idea of *how* the camera works its magic will help you get a higher percentage of good exposures and often opens up additional creative options.

In deciding how much light is needed for correct exposure, your camera employs a light meter that measures the amount of light reflecting from the subject. Taking into account the speed of the film, it then sets the camera's controls for the optimum exposure.

The two basic controls that all cameras use to set exposure are **shutter speed** (the amount of time the film is exposed to light) and **aperture** (the size of the lens opening that lets light into the camera). Shutter speeds are described in fractions of seconds (typically ranging from one second to 1/2,000 second); the fastest speeds let in the least light, and the slowest

let in the most. Apertures are described as numbered *f*/stops; lower-numbered stops (*f*/2.8, for example) let in the most light, and higher-numbered stops (*f*/22) provide the least. In combination, shutter speed and aperture are the gatekeepers that regulate the amount of light that gets to the film.

Understanding the significance of the numerical sequences of each control isn't important. It is important, however, to know that the two controls have an entirely reciprocal relationship: if you open the lens by one aperture stop to let in more light (going from *f*/11 to *f*/8, for example) and then speed up the shutter speed by one stop (from 1/125 to 1/250), you get *exactly the same exposure*. It doesn't matter if you (or the camera) open the lens and speed up the shutter or vice versa: The exposure remains the same. The only difference is that faster shutter speeds stop action better, and changes in aperture affect depth of field (see page 168).

Focal Points

- **Exposure is the amount of light that reaches the film**
- **Shutter speeds regulate how long light hits the film**
- **Aperture is the size of the lens opening**

Exposure and Metering Modes

Getting correct exposure with most simple auto-exposure cameras is easy: press the shutter button and the camera does the rest. More technologically evolved (i.e., expensive) cameras often provide a choice of several exposure and metering modes. Having to maneuver through a labyrinth of optional modes may seem somewhat antiautomatic at first, but in reality they enable you to become the master of, rather than a slave to, automation.

Exposure modes. A choice of different exposure modes enables you to manipulate the camera's selection of shutter speeds and apertures to match a particular type of subject: you can tell it to pick a fast shutter speed because you're photographing a race horse, for instance. Generally, the more costly the camera, the more modes you'll have to choose from, but these are the most common options:

In *Program Mode,* you accept the role of technological slave and the camera selects both the shutter speed and the aperture for you. It is often called the green mode because it's frequently marked by a green "P" on the mode-selector dial. The camera will choose a shutter speed that is safe enough for hand holding

and an aperture that will provide a moderate amount of depth of field. It's ideal for shooting relatively stationary subjects (like a tall ship sitting at anchor) that don't require either a very fast (or slow) shutter speed or excessive (or excessively shallow) depth of field.

In *shutter-priority mode* you choose the shutter speed and the camera selects an appropriate corresponding aperture. If you want to blur the water rushing over a waterfall, for example, you can select a very slow shutter speed and the camera will choose the correct aperture. Conversely, if you want to halt a bounding terrier in mid stride, you can pick a fast shutter speed and, again, the camera will select an appropriate aperture.

The *aperture priority mode,* as you've no doubt guessed, lets you pick the aperture, while the camera selects the matching shutter speed. This is the mode to choose when you want to manipulate depth of field. For example, you could set a small aperture for extensive depth of field (in a landscape, for example) or a large one when you want to limit depth (as in a portrait).

Metering modes allow you to control what part of a scene the

164

meter will take its reading from—an extremely useful capability when it comes to getting good exposure in difficult lighting situations.

Averaging meters, as their name implies, simply average all of the bright and dark areas in a scene to provide an "average" exposure. If the range of brights and darks in a scene is modest, averaging meters provide good exposure. Problems arise when a scene contains particularly large areas of either bright or dark subject matter (see page 166), which can fool the metering system. Most averaging meters overcome this handicap by also using a center-weighted design that gives added emphasis to the center section of the viewfinder, which is, not coincidentally, where most of us put the important subject matter. If you aim the center section at this important part of your subject, excluding dark or bright areas, the meter can calculate a more accurate setting.

Spot meters, a more sophisticated version of center-weighted meters, take their readings from an even smaller section of the viewfinder— often just a few degrees of the total view. Spot meters are an ideal solution in situations where you want to meter a very small area of one tone against a large area of brightness or shadow—a person's face surrounded by bright sky, for example.

Matrix metering or evaluative systems, by far the most sophisticated type of metering wizardry, are eerily accurate even in the most confounding situations. They work by dividing the viewing area into a series of key zones and taking separate readings from each area. This information is then fed into a computer chip that has been programmed with hundreds of thousands of potential lighting combinations; the meter then makes an educated guess at what the important parts of your scene are and exposes accordingly.

Exposing for Dark and Light Subjects

If built-in exposure meters are as omniscient and sophisticated as camera manufacturers claim, why do people still get poorly exposed pictures? The truth is that while most built-in meters are fabulously accurate, they can be fooled. Fortunately, there are ways to wrestle difficult subjects into submission—provided you can recognize a difficult situation.

Light meters are calibrated to give you good exposure for subjects of average brightness; fortunately, most outdoor subjects *are* of average brightness. Problems pop up when you want to photograph subjects that are much lighter or darker than average. Rather than recording such scenes as you see them, the camera will see—and record—them as a medium tone. Instead of pristine white snow, you'll get a drab gray winter wonderland; instead of an inky-black horse, you'll get a gray nag.

If your subject is nearby or very large, the simplest solution is to take a close-up reading and then adjust the exposure using your exposure-compensation dial (or manually) by a stop or two. In photographing the swan (at right), for example, I took a direct reading of the swan and then

added 1½ stops of exposure. This recorded the swan as white and still cast the water into blackness. Had I been photographing a black bull in a meadow, I would have taken a reading from the animal and *subtracted* one to two stops of exposure to keep it black.

The problem gets more tedious when you are photographing a relatively small average-toned subject against a very dark or light background—a friend lying on a bright sandy beach, for instance. The best recourse here is to use your spot-metering mode and take a reading of just the subject. This way at least your main subject will be correctly exposed, even if, because of the contrast, you lose some detail in the background. Yet another solution is to scout the scene for something of average brightness—green foliage is good—and set your exposure for that.

Focal Points

- **Meters are fooled by very light or dark subjects**
- **Try a stop or two of exposure compensation**
- **Spot-meter to read subjects on light or dark backgrounds**

Controlling Depth of Field

The topic of depth of field (DOF) tends to give the shakes to many beginning photographers, but the concept is actually very simple. It is the range in a scene, from near to far, that is in sharp focus. The ability to control how much is in focus has an immense effect on your pictures. When shooting a landscape, for example, you'll want as much of the photograph in sharp focus as possible, so a significant depth of field is required. In other situations, as in taking a portrait, a shallower area of sharp focus will isolate your subject from distracting backgrounds.

Three things control how great the depth of field will be in a photograph: lens focal length, aperture, and distance from the subject. Other things being equal, shorter-focal-length lenses, smaller apertures, and greater lens-to-subject distance all increase the range of sharp focus, while longer lenses, wider apertures, and a shorter distance to your subject shrink depth of field.

When you look through your lens, however, you will not be seeing what's really sharp and what's not. With point-and-shoot cameras, this is because you're not looking through the lens—you're looking through a separate viewfinder. With SLRs, you're looking through the lens at its widest aperture; it closes to a smaller f/stop only at the instant you press the shutter button. This is a problem if you're using a medium telephoto lens to take a portrait of Mom in gay Paree. As you look through the lens, it *appears* that the traffic and crowds in the background are out of focus. But because you have a small aperture set, when you get the picture back, zingo, Mom is lost in all that junk behind her.

The solution? Many SLRs have a depth-of-field preview button; when you press it, the lens briefly closes to the shooting aperture, showing you the real depth of field. Be aware that when you press this button, the image in the viewfinder will temporarily darken. If too much is in focus, simply open the aperture, put on a longer lens, or move closer. Or all three. If too little is sharp? Well, you can figure that out.

Focal Points

- **Depth of field is the range of sharp focus in a picture**
- **Lens focal length, aperture, and distance all affect DOF**
- **SLRs with a DOF preview let you see what's in sharp focus**

Lenses

Lenses are the eyes through which your camera sees the world. You can change the way your camera sees simply by changing lenses. Matching the right lens to the right subject is one of the ultimate keys to creative photography. Knowing how to do this is a matter of experience and of understanding the basic characteristics of different types of lenses.

All lenses are described in two ways: by their focal length (as measured in millimeters) and by their speed (jargon for their maximum aperture). A 300 mm *f*/2.8 lens has a focal length of 300 mm and a speed of *f*/2.8. The focal length of a lens is important, because it gives you an idea of how its angle-of-view and perspective relate to our own vision of the world. Lenses of about 50 mm, for example, are considered *normal* because they provide approximately the same angle-of-view and perspective that our eyes see. Lenses shorter than 50 mm are considered *wide-angle* lenses; those longer than normal are considered *telephoto* or long lenses.

170

Lens speed indicates how bright the image in the viewfinder will be. Lenses with larger maximum apertures (see page 162) provide a

brighter viewfinder image but are not necessarily sharper or better than slower lenses. Their main advantage is that they provide better viewing in dimly lighted situations. For example, a 200 mm *f*/2.8 lens (considered very fast for that long a lens) would produce a brighter viewing image than a 200 mm *f*/4. As a rule, lenses with wider maximum apertures are more expensive.

Normal lenses provide about the same perspective as the human eye and are usually in the 45 mm-to-60 mm range for 35 mm cameras. Not too many years ago, your first lens was always a normal lens—SLRs often came with them whether you wanted them or not. Today they are less in favor, largely because most people buy zoom lenses (which often include the normal range) as their first lens. Still, I find that normal lenses offer a straightforward view of the world that is particularly well suited to travel, and I wouldn't travel without one. Many also double as macro (close-up) lenses—very useful.

Wide-angle lenses are superb at reaching out their wide-open optical arms to take in sweeping views of the world. Those in the 20 mm-to-35 mm range are the most popular, 35

mm being the focal length that many point-and-shoot cameras come with. Creatively, they can be used to heighten perspective by exaggerating the distance between near and far objects or, when you're shooting upward, the height of nearby ones. Wide-angle lenses are well suited to numerous subjects, including landscapes, architecture, and situations where shooting space is tight. They also provide inherently greater depth of field (see page 168) than other lenses.

Telephoto lenses have focal lengths that range from about 85 mm (good for portraits) to supertelephotos' 300 mm to 600 mm or longer. All telephoto lenses bring distant subjects (like wildlife) closer; the longer the focal length, the greater the magnification. They also effectively compress space—cramming a city skyline into an overlapping pattern of geometric shapes, for instance. Unfortunately, as focal length increases, lenses become bigger, heavier, slower, and more expensive. You have to measure the need for a longer lens

against its cost and inconvenience.

Zoom lenses have a variable focal length and are by far the most popular lenses on the market today—with good reason. Instead of carrying a normal, a wide-angle, and a telephoto lens, you can get one lens that covers the range from 28 mm to 105 mm. Add a second zoom in the 80 mm-to-210 mm range to cover your telephoto needs, and you have an extremely broad choice of focal lengths in just two lenses. The other exciting aspect of zooms, of course, is that they let you alter your composition without changing your shooting position—a major convenience, especially when you're traveling. The flip side is that zooms are slower than single-focal-length lenses, and I have never found the zoom that matches their sharpness or contrast—manufacturers' claims notwithstanding.

Focal Points

- **Use wide-angle lenses to take in wide views**
- **Use telephoto lenses to bring distant subjects near**
- **Get many lenses in one with a zoom**

Creative Filters

You can have fun using creative filters to jazz up or create a specific mood in your photographs, but they're most effective if used sparingly. Too many filtered pictures will make your travel album look like a trip to a special-effects theme park. Filters come in two types: plastic or glass squares that slip into a holder, or glass discs that screw to your lens. Either is fine; just be sure they're of good quality, so that they don't degrade image sharpness.

Soft-focus or diffusion filters give a misty quality to images and can impart a romantic mood to scenics and flower close-ups. They're also good for portraits; they soften wrinkles and skin blemishes, so your vainer travel companions will think you're a brilliant photographer. These filters come in various levels of intensity, but stick with milder ones. Diffusion filters work best at wide apertures; too small an f/stop increases depth of field and defeats the softening effect.

Colored filters come in almost every color you can imagine (and some you can't). Think of the fun of turning the canals of Venice tangerine or capturing a friend's face in a lovely shade of magenta. Colored filters are interesting to play with but

have little useful value. I sometimes use yellow or orange filters to intensify less-than-spectacular sunsets, but even these grow redundant after a few shots.

Split-field-density filters have a graduated area of color (or density) across the surface of the filter. Neutral filters are good for holding back bright areas of sky so you can expose properly for a darker foreground; they typically come in one-, two-, and three-stop densities. Colored graduates do the same thing but add a tinge of color to the sky—you often see this effect in magazine advertisements. The best split-field filters are rectangular ones that slip into a lens-mounted frame so you can position the area of density.

Star filters create pretty patterns from point-light sources, such as light bulbs, candles, or sparkles on water. Typically they come in four-, six-, and eight-point configurations; I used a four-pointer to shoot the cruise ship at night (opposite, top).

Focal Points

- **Use creative filters sparingly**
- **Stick with mild diffusion filters**
- **Save colored filters for play**
- **Use split-field-density filters to expose for a dark foreground**

Polarizing Filters

If you use an SLR, the single most helpful accessory you can own, other than a tripod, is a polarizing filter. This seemingly simple bit of glass that screws to your lens in a rotating mount performs a host of remarkable photographic feats, including darkening blue skies, removing reflections, and increasing color contrast and saturation. *How* it works is a seminar in the physics of light, but using one is simple: All you do is turn the filter until you see the effect you want in the viewfinder, and then shoot.

Polarizers are most commonly used to darken blue skies in outdoor and scenic photographs by cutting through atmospheric haze. They work with both color and black-and-white films to create a striking contrast between deep sky and white clouds. Sky-darkening works, however, only when the sun is at about 90 degrees from the angle you're facing; in other words, it must be to your left or right or overhead, but not behind or in front of you. Nor does the effect work on overcast days. Take care to use sky-darkening in moderation; too much saturation can make skies look ominous and unnatural.

Polarizers are also handy for removing reflections from nonmetallic surfaces, like glass or water. If you're trying to shoot a store-window display (as in the photos at bottom right) or little fish in a tidal pool, just turn the filter until the reflections vanish. The effect works best when you are at about a 35-degree angle to the reflecting surface. You can even use a polarizer to remove the myriad infinitesimal bits of reflection and glare in outdoor scenes, making subjects like foliage and grass vibrant and rich with color.

The only drawback to using polarizing filters is that they do absorb some light—usually about 1⅓ stops. Most through-the-lens meters will compensate for the lost light, but be sure you are using the right type of filter. Manual-focus cameras use a *linear* polarizer, while many autofocus cameras use a *circular* version. Check your camera manual to be sure.

Focal Points

- **Use polarizing filters to increase contrast**
- **Use polarizing filters to erase reflections on nonmetallic surfaces**
- **Use the right filter**

Motion

The idea in photographing most action subjects (see page 34) is to use a shutter speed that's fast enough to stop any hint of motion. There are times, though, when intentionally switching to a slow shutter speed and exaggerating subject movement better interprets its true essence. A race horse frozen in mid-stride is not nearly as expressive of action as one whose four legs are tangled in a rhythmic blur.

One way to capture action in motion is by keeping the camera steady and letting the movement write its own story across the frame. In photographing a rush-hour crowd, for example, standing in one place and using a long exposure will turn the onslaught into a swirling array of faceless forms. As with stopping action, the actual shutter speed you use will depend on three factors: the speed of your subject, its direction, and how close it is. As a starting point, estimate the correct shutter speed for stopping action and then experiment with shutter speeds at least two times slower; typically speeds in the 1/30- to 1/4-second range are effective.

In the technique called panning, you use a slow shutter speed and move

the camera to follow your subject. The result is a relatively sharp subject surrounded by a blurred or streaked background. With a moderately slow shutter speed (1/60 or slower), focus on your subject (a skier, say) and gently press the shutter as you pan with it. It helps if there's a good color contrast between subject and background (see page 80). Panning is one technique for which a point-and-shoot has an advantage, because you can continue to see your subject during the exposure. With an SLR, once you press the shutter, the reflex mirror will block your view.

Occasionally *you* may be the one in motion—trying to shoot pictures from a moving cable car, for example. In these situations stopping action (not to mention camera-shake) is near impossible, and it's often better simply to go with the flow, slow down the shutter speed, and let some blur into your pictures.

Focal Points

- **Blur to capture the feel of motion**

- **Use a slow shutter speed to let the subject blur**

- **To pan, follow a moving subject with the camera**

Lights in Motion

A night-related special effect that often appears in travel-magazine photos and is easy to mimic involves taking long time exposures of lights in motion. Because film has the unique ability to record the paths of moving lights, it can reveal patterns and designs of light that are entirely invisible to the eye. Unfortunately, you can use the technique only if your camera has a shutter that you can lock open or that lets you set very long exposure times (10 seconds or longer).

My favorite subject for light streaking is the swirling trails of automobile head- and taillights. It's a great way to brighten up city street scenes, especially when you shoot from a high enough vantage point to reveal an elaborate traffic pattern or when you include a landmark, such as the Arc de Triomphe, as a focal point. One curious aspect of this technique is that, while the film perfectly records the glow of headlights and taillights, the cars are moving too fast to be recorded, so they disappear. Taking an exposure reading for traffic lights is all but impossible, so your best bet is simply to set a small aperture (f/11 or smaller) to give you adequate depth of field, then keep the shutter open long enough for the lights to move all

the way through the frame. I've used exposures of from 10 seconds to several minutes.

You can use the same technique to photograph carnival or amusement-park rides in motion. Ferris wheels and other spinning rides are especially attractive, because their colorful light displays form dramatic swirls of light. To get the complete-circle effect, you have to be sure to shoot at least one revolution of the ride. A good way to do this is to pick a spot on the wheel, wait until it hits the twelve-o'clock point, then keep the shutter open until it passes that point again.

Remember, these are experimental techniques, so it's a good idea to shoot lots of film and bracket widely.

Focal Points

- **Try long exposures to capture paths of moving lights**
- **Shoot traffic patterns with several-second exposures**
- **Experiment and shoot lots of film**

The Zoom Effect

In addition to offering you the marvelous convenience of being able to change focal lengths quickly between pictures, zoom lenses enable you to create a novel special effect by changing focal lengths *during* an exposure. The result of this zoom effect is a relatively sharp central subject engulfed in a radiant burst of light streaks. The effect works best with a strong color or tonal contrast or with a brightly colored subject set against a dark background.

With a slow-speed (ISO 64 or slower) film, take a meter reading of your subject using your shutter-priority- (or manual-) exposure mode. The effect is most pronounced when you zoom through the entire focal range, so choose a relatively slow shutter speed—preferably ⅛ second or longer. To make the exposure, simply press the shutter button with one hand and slide or twist the zoom through its focal range with the other. Coordinating your two hands on the two controls takes some practice, but the slower the shutter speed, the more time you have to unravel the logistics.

Using a tripod is a necessity, because you're going to need both hands to operate camera controls and because

once you begin the exposure, the reflex mirror of your SLR will be locked up, blocking your view of the subject. It's also simpler to compose the picture if you zoom from the longest focal-length setting (telephoto) to the widest (wide-angle); that way you know for sure what will be in the center of your frame.

Once you are comfortable working with stationary subjects in broad daylight, try something a little more challenging, like a sports-action shot. The added dynamics of the zoom streaks intensify the impression of speed and motion. Night shots, like the city overview shown here, are also powerful—as you zoom, each little droplet of light becomes a scintillating trail of color.

Focal Points

- **Use zoom for subjects with strong contrasts**
- **Keep the main subject centered**
- **Zoom from telephoto to wide-angle**

Multiple Exposures

By making more than one exposure on a single frame of film, you can create outlandish and visually striking images. The exposures can be related thematically (a sailboat over a pretty sunset, for example), or they can simply fit together into an arresting graphic design. Many SLR and some point-and-shoot cameras have multiple-exposure buttons that make creating such pictures simple; on some older SLRs, you may be able to override the film advance by holding in the rewind button while you recock the shutter.

Creating an effective multiple exposure takes some planning; you should visualize the final image before you begin the exposure sequence. You could just photograph a mountain range and then run around looking for something else to superimpose on it, but what if another great single-exposure shot comes along while you're looking? Better to know exactly what each exposure will be and then shoot them quickly in sequence. Try to think in terms of layers—for example, a close-up of shells and a silhouette of a lone palm tree as the second layer.

My favorite double-exposure technique is the one I used to make the shot of the pink gingerbread

cottage on Martha's Vineyard at right. I first took a sharply focused picture of the cottage with my camera on a tripod; then, without moving the camera, I twisted the lens until the cottage was completely out of focus and shot the second exposure. The combination of sharp and soft epitomizes, for me, the fanciful romance of the scene.

Whenever you make two or more exposures on a single frame, you must adjust the exposure or the film will be overexposed. Some auto-exposure cameras make this compensation automatically; on others you have to do it manually. As a basic rule, you should *decrease* exposure by one stop for each exposure you add. If you make a double exposure, for example, decrease the exposure for each by one stop below what the meter recommends.

184

Focal Points

- **Plan ahead**
- **Think in layers**
- **Decrease exposure by one stop for each additional exposure**

Right Light, Wrong Film

Color films are designed to be used with either daylight or incandescent indoor light (tungsten), and they provide the most accurate color results when matched with the lighting. By deliberately using the wrong film with a particular light source, you can capture images that have either an exaggerated coolness or an enhanced warmth to them. Many photographers discover the effect quite by accident when they change light sources but not film.

Our eyes and brain adjust quickly to changes in color of lighting and accept almost any light source as neutral (or "white") after just a few moments. Films, like Mr. Spock, are logical and truthful to the bitter end—they see and record light as it is. Daylight films are balanced for the approximate color of sunlight on a clear day. Incandescent lamps are warmer, or more reddish, in color than daylight; if you use a daylight film with incandescent lamps, you will be exaggerating the reddish cast of the lighting. This can be very

useful if you want to heighten the warmth or coziness of an indoor scene—a portrait of a friend reading by lamplight, for instance. Using daylight film with tungsten lights is also good for heightening the mood of pictures where there is already some existing source of warmth, such as candlelight.

Indoor film used outdoors has the opposite effect. The additional blue bias included in the film's emulsion (to correct for the reddish color of incandescent lights) records outdoor scenes with an exaggerated coolness. Daylight scenes (as in the shot at right), especially those containing snow or water, appear to be bathed in moonlight. Underexposing by one to two stops intensifies the effect. Incidentally, this is how Hollywood creates day-as-night scenes.

It's best to use color slide films for this technique, because the color balance of negative films is often corrected in the printing stage.

Focal Points

- **Use daylight film indoors for a cozy, warm atmosphere**
- **Use tungsten-balanced films outdoors for a moonlit look**
- **Use color slide films, not color negative films**

Film

You can simplify your decision about what kind of film to bring on a trip if you consider what you want as a final product and what conditions you are likely to be shooting in.

To shoot in color, you must decide first whether you want to use color negative or color slide (also called color transparency) film. **Color negative films** are made for color prints and enlargements; their prime advantage is that they tolerate moderate amounts of color correction during the printing stage. They are also forgiving of exposure errors; you can be off a stop or more and still have acceptable prints.

Professionals prefer **color slide films** because most commercial reproduction is done from transparencies. Transparencies are not forgiving of exposure error and cannot be color corrected, as there is no printing stage. You can, however, have color prints and enlargements made from slide films.

Films also vary according to their **ISO number** or **film speed**: their sensitivity to light. The higher a film's ISO number, the more responsive or "faster" it is; thus, an ISO 400 film is faster than an ISO 100 film. If you plan to do most of your shooting in bright tropical sunlight, then a film

speed of ISO 64 will suffice; indoors or in dim situations outdoors, you'll need a faster film— typically ISO 400 or more. Each doubling (or halving) of the speed is equal to one stop of light; an ISO 400 film, for instance, is twice as fast as an ISO 200 film, or one stop more sensitive, and vice versa.

Color films are **color balanced** to be used with a specific type of light (see also page 186). Color negative film is daylight-balanced, but if you will be shooting in a variety of indoor and outdoor lighting conditions, it's still the best choice, because you can correct in the printing stage for odd color shifts. Color slide films are available in both daylight and tungsten balance; if accurate color is required, you should match the film to the light source.

All black-and-white films are negative films, so with them the choice is mainly film speed.

Focal Points

- **Choose color negative film to get color prints**

- **Use color slide film for transparencies**

- **Select an ISO film speed to match lighting conditions**

Creating a
Travel Journal

7

The Travel Journal

The pictures you take on a trip should add up to more than a shoeboxful of random glimpses of a place. They should incorporate, if not a formal storyline, at least a certain continuity or chronological progression. Any journey has a start, a middle, and a finish; whether you arrange your pictures in an album or project them in a slide show, they will be more meaningful to you and interesting to others if they express that framework.

Keeping track of where and when you shot each picture will help in organizing them when you get home. If your camera has a data back that date-stamps your pictures, turn the date stamp on for the first and last few shots of each roll to set up date parameters for those pictures. I always bring blank removable labels and mark each film canister with the subject(s) as I unload it from the camera. When I get home, I simply transfer those labels to the processing pouch as they go out; my pictures are then organized by date and place before I even see them.

Logistics aside, it's important to give your journal elements of both visual surprise and emotional discovery. In the same way that motion pictures have lulls leading to dramatic

moments that lead to higher crescendos and then settle down to quieter interludes, so can your photographs. Mixing up views of recognizable landmarks with interesting detail shots and portraits will provide visual variety, too. Try to mix ordinary scenes—breakfast by the pool—with your more spectacular aerial shots of Angel Falls. Another strong device is to create a running theme, whether it's humorous signs (see page 206) or the faces of new friends.

Finally, don't be afraid to jazz up your photo album with other photographers' work or trip mementoes. I often add postcards, restaurant napkins, and other paper paraphernalia to my albums.

Focal Points

- **Tell a story with your travel pictures**

- **Label films while traveling with date and location**

- **Create a mix of scenics, close-ups and people shots**

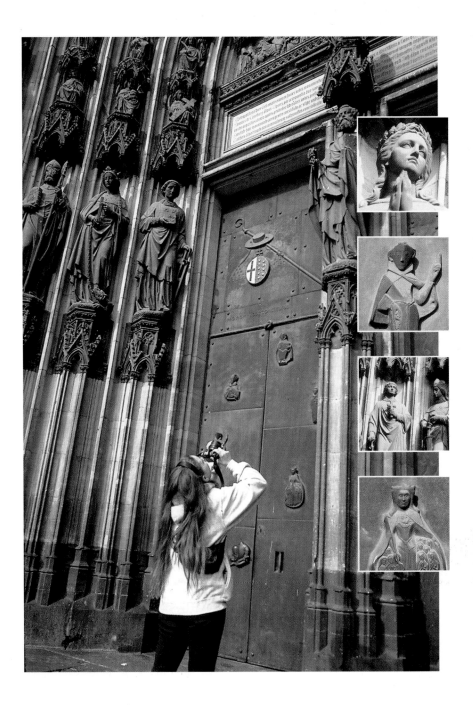

Catherine Karnow:
In the Grenadines

Regatta boat, Bequia. "All of a sudden, the sun squeezed through a cloud, and there was this fabulous light. I was using a 20 mm lens; very wide and very

Photo P. Lichfield

Born and raised in Hong Kong, the daughter of an American journalist, San Francisco–based photographer Catherine Karnow is a woman whose life seems destined to have travel at its center. She moved to Washington, D.C., at age ten and first developed a serious interest in photography in high school; it was then that she began spending her summers abroad photographing. After a brief career as a filmmaker, she turned to still photography. Though she has been working professionally full time for only six years, she has rapidly become one of the world's most sought-after travel photographers. Her work appears frequently in *Smithsonian, GEO, Figaro,* and *Islands;* and she has participated in several Day in the Life book projects, including *A Day in the Life of Hollywood.* Karnow was among 70 of the world's leading photojournalists chosen to work on the book *A Passage to Vietnam*, the critically acclaimed photographic study of the country—the project of which she says she is the most proud. Her other book projects have included the *Insight Guides* to France, Provence, Los Angeles, and Washington, D.C. She has also worked extensively in Scotland and the Caribbean. The following portfolio was shot while she was on assignment in the Grenadine Islands.

close. I wanted to get the looming effect, so you feel you're racing against the boat—you're in the race."

Tobago Cays (above). "Aerials are wonderful to do in the Caribbean because the water looks so amazing and there are such different forms to the islands."

Keith St. Bernard, Grenada (opposite, above). "I shot this walking side-by-side with him—we were both moving."

Model builder, Bequia (left). "I like finding local artists wherever I go; Bequia is known for its model boat makers."

Nutmegs and mace, Bay Gardens, Grenada (opposite, left). "This is a good way to do what is in effect a still life—to have a person holding the subject."

Windward village, Carriacou (opposite, right).

Tobago Cays (right).

Cattle boat, Hillsborough Bay, Carriacou (below). "You can get a good picture anytime, anywhere. I got this one while I was hanging around waiting for somebody."

Just-caught fish (opposite). "In a split second they were hauling up this fish and pouring rum over it to stun it, and I was ready with my camera."

Mopion Island, near Union Island (right). "I just love this picture because it's really subtle—there's a little puff of cloud right above her head."

Gingerbread Houses, Mustique (left). "I actually shot these with full sun but didn't like them, so I came back when the light was gentler. The bright sun made the houses look too garish."

Man cleaning pool, Mustique (above). "I spent time with the people who own and rent the villas and I got nice pictures of them, but I felt it was important to show the other people who make up the population of the island."

Staff bringing cocktails, Petit St. Vincent (far left). "I set up this shot so I could work with the situation and shoot it with different lenses."

Researching Your Trip

One of the most important aspects of photographing a trip has nothing to do with cameras or lenses or film; it is the time you spend researching before you go. Studying a place and planning a shooting itinerary will vastly enhance the number and quality of the photo opportunities you encounter. You probably won't get to every idea on your list, but at least you won't miss any hidden gems. How awful it would be to drive from Phoenix to Flagstaff in Arizona and not make the 20-minute side trip into lovely Sedona because you didn't know it was there! Or to plan a winter trip to South America and miss a carnival by choosing the wrong week.

The best way to learn about a place is to read everything you can find about it. Travel magazines, Sunday newspaper travel sections, and, of course, guidebooks are terrific sources of practical information and ideas. Another indispensable source of information is the public library. Chances are yours will have atlases, books, and journals offering details about commerce, weather, geography, and holidays that will lead to dozens of picture ideas. If you're traveling to a place where you don't speak the language, many libraries lend language tapes that can help you learn some basic phrases.

The best sources of information on a place are people who have been there. People love to tell you where they've been; the minute you bring up a locale, someone will share his or her own adventure with you. If you're of a more high-tech nature, most on-line computer services have lively electronic travel bulletin boards—often you can reach people in the places you're planning to visit.

201

Focal Points

- **Study books and maps and visit the library**

- **Make a tentative list of picture ideas**

- **Talk to other people who have visited your destination**

From the Land and Sea

On almost any trip, you'll find yourself using all sorts of ground and sea transportation. Depending on where you roam, your transport may range from the ultramodern, like the high-speed trains of Japan, to the traditional, like the eccentric jitneys of the Philippines or the gondolas of Venice. Photographs of and from these conveyances bring a great sense of presence and authenticity to travel pictures that helps carry the viewer along on your journey.

En route, your transportation will often reveal vistas or vignettes that you may not see again once you arrive at your destination, so be sure you have a camera ready to snatch such opportunities. Point-and-shoot cameras are ideal for this kind of photography, because they let you react quickly with little fuss or bother. One solution to the problem of constant motion is to use high-speed films (ISO 400 or faster), so that you can set shutter speeds fast enough to stop the motion and f/stops small enough to provide adequate depth of field. The alternative is to use a slow film and intentionally set a slow shutter speed (see page 178) to present a blurred, more vivid impression of movement.

Once you arrive in a place, take time to look around for interesting views that include your means of transportation. Straight shots of a ship in a harbor or a train at the station tend to be static, so try instead to find compositions that reveal their relationship to the locale. After arriving by cruise ship in Bermuda, I was walking up a hill several blocks away from the port when I turned back and saw just how overwhelming the ship was in the context of the two-story storefronts along the harbor. I hiked around until I found a clear shot of the ship's bow, then captured both ship and stores with a wide-angle lens. I took the shot of the ferry (opposite, bottom left) while commuting across the Rhine between my hotel and a convention center. It was a unique experience that I wanted to record for my album.

202

Focal Points

- **Shoot pictures of your transportation**

- **Keep a point-and-shoot handy for en-route pictures**

- **Include photos of depots, harbors, or stations**

From the Air

One of the reasons I love to fly is that I am absolutely fascinated by the view of the Earth from the window of a plane. It doesn't matter where I'm flying or whether it's day or night: As long as we're not flying through clouds or fog, my eyes are glued to the window. I'm always thrilled when I get a chatty pilot who likes to identify the sights along the way. The first time I heard one say you could see the Grand Canyon from the left side of the plane, I nearly leapt over the person in the window seat to get a peek. Now I *always* request a window seat.

Pictures taken from commercial airliners won't be perfect technically, because the plastic windows are so thick they destroy sharpness. Still, the quality is fine for 4- × 6-inch album prints. You can minimize the blurring by getting the lens as close to the window as possible, but avoid

touching the surface or fuselage, because the plane's vibration will cause camera shake. Take-offs and landings are the best time to shoot, because the lower altitude makes ground features more recognizable and there's less haze.

In many places you can take relatively inexpensive low-altitude air tours to get some one-of-a-kind scenery shots. Most of the planes have high wings, and often the pilots will let you pop open the window to get clean photos if they know you're a serious shooter. A normal or mild wide-angle lens is good for both commercial and low-level tour planes, but you can use longer lenses to isolate smaller ground features from an open window. In all cases, I've found that the exposure recommended by my through-the-lens meter is very accurate. Depth of field doesn't matter, so use the highest shutter speed you can to offset vibration.

204

Focal Points

- **Reserve a window seat on commmercial planes**
- **Keep the lens close to but not against the window**
- **Shoot during take-offs and landings**

Signs Along the Way

At home we take most signs for granted, barely noticing them unless they happen to be lit up in pink neon, mention a monetary fine, or provide directions. On the road, especially in more exotic parts of the world, spotting interesting signs is great fun; you can use them as a running theme in a travel journal. Pictures of signs can identify locales, mark progress, provide information, or even just make people laugh.

Humor is always successful, especially when it is unintended and comes from juxtaposition or odd coincidence. At a trade show in Germany, I noticed that the signs for rest rooms were always posted next to signs featuring a silhouette of a man running. It took me a few double-takes to realize that the latter were pointing out emergency exits, not patrons in dire biological straits. Together, the two signs made a great souvenir snap.

Familiar-looking signs in other languages, such as a French stop sign saying ARRET, are also attention grabbers. If you're traveling in a place where languages change frequently, as in Europe, try building a collection of similar signs in several languages. I've always been fascinated by Asian calligraphy,

especially when there's a lot of it lit up in neon in places like Hong Kong. I have no idea what the signs I'm shooting say, but they make very graphic images.

Probably the most useful exploitation of signs is to mark progress in your travel album. Look especially for signs that announce dramatic locales (as in the sign for the equator at right), city limits, unusual town names, or driving distances. Signs that recall trip highlights, such as hotel banners or names of famous museums, are also useful as props or backgrounds for posing your companions. Photographing historical markers, if you can read the language, is a good way to remember details of a historic place or event.

Focal Points

- **Use pictures of signs in your album**

- **Keep an eye open for humorous or foreign-language signs**

- **Use signs to show your trip's progress**

Photographing Your Cruise

The first time I took a cruise, I had no choice but to create a travel journal of the trip: I was on a photographic assignment to do just that. One key thing I learned during that voyage was that you have to be prepared to work in a lot of different lighting situations: on deck in very bright sunlight, indoors by dim available light, and in both good and bad weather (yes, it does rain on cruise vacations).

One of the blessings of cruising is that you can bring a ton of gear and it's as near as your cabin. If you are an SLR shooter, bring a pair of zooms (a wide-angle-to-normal and a telephoto zoom), an accessory flash, and both fast and slow films. I found myself shooting ISO 25 film on deck at midday and taking night shots with ISO 400 or 1000 film. I also brought a point-and-shoot for taking informal snaps at places like the midnight buffet (where carrying an SLR would have interfered with my eating everything in sight).

If you're making an inland passage or are cruising in an island group like the Bahamas, you'll have many opportunities to photograph scenery from on deck. Coming into port is an especially exciting time, but it happens quickly and often at dawn,

so be up early and bring everything you need. Work from the upper decks and use a wide lens to include the bow or side of the ship for scale and perspective. On breezy days there will be a windward (windy) and leeward (calm) side to the ship; if the scenery is equally nice, shoot from the latter.

Most ships publish a daily calendar that is slipped under your door each night by seagoing elves; it lists the next day's events and helps you plan your day's shooting. On a ship you don't have to worry about not being included in pictures; the ship's photographers will capture your group's every waking moment and post the photos for sale each evening.

Focal Points

- **Take along films with a variety of speeds**
- **Shoot scenics from on deck with a wide-angle**
- **Use fast films or flash to shoot shipboard activites**

Travel Hints

Traveling with film and camera equipment presents few problems besides having one more thing to carry, but here are some quick tips to make life easier:

X-ray machines have been the dread of photographers since they first came into use in airports. Recent studies, though, have shown that even frequent exposure to well-maintained X-ray machines in developed countries does little or no damage to films. Machines in undeveloped and smaller countries are not as carefully monitored. The exception to this is very fast films (ISO 400 and faster), because their added sensitivity makes them more susceptible to potential damage. Remember, too, that X-ray damage is cumulative; one or two doses will do no harm, even to fast films. If, however, you are at all concerned, pack your film in clear zipper-lock plastic bags and ask for hand inspection. Be aware, though, that while the FAA requires security personnel in United States airports to hand-inspect film, you're at the whim of the officials in other countries. Be polite and patient, arrive early, and most will accommodate you.

Checking equipment through with your luggage when you fly is lethal

for the equipment. With the exception of a small point-and-shoot wrapped lovingly in a thick wool sweater in the *center* of a suitcase, I would *never* check photo gear or film. If the luggage crusher doesn't get it, some opportunist thief will. Carry it with you.

How much film you bring really depends on your shooting habits. Some people never shoot more than two rolls a day; I shoot an average of 10 to 15, often more. Always, but always, bring double the amount you *think* you will need. Film is very expensive in tourist destinations, and it's a major hassle to have to interrupt your touring to go looking for it.

Batteries are often impossible to find on the road, so always bring an extra or two. Most cameras are useless without them.

Customs and other regulations are usually not a problem, but some countries limit the amount of film and photo gear you can bring across their borders. Your travel agent can find out. If you are traveling with new equipment, it's a good idea to register it with the United States customs officials at the airport before you go, so you won't have to prove ownership coming home or in other places. Bringing several photocopies of receipts (for film and cameras) is a good idea, too.

Processing abroad is fine (cheaper in some places, more expensive in others) if you are in a very modern country. Check the quality of the prints in developers' displays. I often have a test roll processed just to be sure my cameras are working and to get a sneak peek at how I'm doing. You can make your own postcards, too!

Buying equipment abroad is not a good idea. In the face of currency-exchange rates, duties, and unusable warranty arrangements, you should buy cameras abroad only if the one you bring dies or is lost. For backup you can bring several one-time-use cameras; these are also great if you are making a side trip to someplace where you don't want to risk your real camera—a rafting excursion or rainy-day hike, for example.

Pint-size minitripods are a convenient alternative to carrying a full-size support and provide good stability. They come as small as 6 inches, weigh just a few ounces, and can be rested on vertical as well as horizontal surfaces to steady the camera. Fabric-covered beanbags are another option—particularly useful for resting a long lens on a rock or a car fender.

Further Reading

General

The Art of Seeing, by Derek Doeffinger. Kodak Books, 1988.

Kodak's Most Basic Book of 35 mm Photography, by Jeff Wignall. Kodak Books, 1993.

The Joy of Photography, 3rd ed., by Jeff Wignall (writer) and the Editors of Kodak. Addison-Wesley, 1991.

Learning to See Creatively, by Bryan Peterson. Amphoto, Watson-Guptill, 1988.

Michael Langford's 35 mm Handbook, by Michael Langford. Knopf, 1993.

The Photographer's Handbook, by John Hedgcoe. Knopf, 1993.

Understanding Exposure, by Bryan Peterson. Amphoto, Watson-Guptill, 1990.

Winning Pictures: 101 Ideas for Outstanding Photographs, by Jeff Wignall. Silver Pixel Press, 1995.

Outdoor and Landscape

The African Elephant: Last Days of Eden, by Boyd Norton. Voyageur Press, 1991.

The Art of Outdoor Photography, by Boyd Norton. Voyageur Press, 1993.

The Art of Photographing Nature, by Art Wolfe; text by Martha Hill. Crown, 1993.

Galen Rowell's Vision: The Art of Adventure Photography, by Galen Rowell. Sierra Club Books, 1993.

John Shaw's Landscape Photography, by John Shaw. Amphoto, 1994.

The Mountain Gorilla, by Boyd Norton. Voyageur Press, 1990.

Mountain Light: In Search of the Dynamic Landscape, by Galen Rowell. Sierra Club Books, 1987.

Vineyard Summer, by Alison Shaw. Little, Brown, 1994.

Technical

The Camera, by Ansel Adams. New York Graphic Society, 1980.

The Hasselblad Manual, 4th ed., by Ernst Wildi. Focal Press, 1992.

For further information about rainbows, contact: Rainbow Research Project (c/o Rainbow Vibes, Box 1045, South Norwalk, CT 06856).

Photo Credits

213

Topics

214